Imagine

Winter Edition
2016 Poetry Collection

Imagine represents our student authors as accurately as possible.
Every effort has been made to print each poem
as it was submitted with minimal editing
of spelling, grammar, and punctuation.
All submissions have been formatted to this compilation.

Published by
The America Library of Poetry
P.O. Box 978
Houlton, ME 04730
Website: www.libraryofpoetry.com
Email: generalinquiries@libraryofpoetry.com

Printed in the United States of America.

THE AMERICA
LIBRARY OF POETRY

ISBN: 978-0-9966841-2-5

Contents

Poetry by Division

Foreword

There are two kinds of writers in the world.
There are those who write from experience,
and those who write from imagination.
The experienced, offer words that are a reflection of their lives.
The triumphs they have enjoyed, the heartaches they have endured;
all the things that have made them who they are,
they graciously share with us, as a way of sharing themselves,
and in doing so, give us, as readers, someone to whom we may relate,
as well as fresh new perspectives
on what may be our common circumstances in life.
From the imaginative,
come all the wonderful things we have yet to experience;
from sights unseen, to sounds unheard.
They encourage us to explore the limitless possibilities
of our dreams and fantasies,
and aid us in escaping, if only temporarily,
the confines of reality and the rules of society.
To each, we owe a debt of gratitude;
and rightfully so, as each provides a service of equal importance.
Yet, without the other, neither can be truly beneficial.
For instance, one may succeed in accumulating a lifetime of experience,
only to consider it all to have been predictable and unfulfilling,
if denied the chance to chase a dream or two along the way.
Just as those whose imaginations run away with them never to return,
may find that without solid footing in the real world,
life in fantasyland is empty.
As you now embark, dear reader,
upon your journey through these words to remember,
you are about to be treated to both heartfelt tales of experience,
and captivating adventures of imagination.
It is our pleasure to present them for your enjoyment.
To our many authors,
who so proudly represent the two kinds of writers in the world,
we dedicate this book, and offer our sincere thanks;
for now, possibly more than ever,
the world needs you both.

Paul Wilson Charles
Editor

Editor's Choice Award

The Editor's Choice Award is presented
to an author who demonstrates not only
the solid fundamentals of creative writing,
but also the ability to elicit an emotional response
or provide a thought provoking body of work
in a manner which is both clear and concise.

You will find "A Season For Blueberries"
by Wilson Haims on page 201 of Imagine

2016
Winter Edition
Spirit of Education
For Outstanding Participation

Blacksburg Elementary School

Blacksburg, South Carolina

Presented to participating students and faculty
in recognition of your commitment
to literary excellence.

Division I

Grades
3-5

Life
by Romi Landreth

Life needs to be spent well,
And have every moment cherished.
It needs to have meaning,
It needs to be full.
It needs to have love,
And heartache.
Life has good and life has bad,
And if you look for the good in things,
Then that is what you will have.
If there was no life,
There would be no Earth.
No humans, nor animals or plants.
When life comes to an end,
Another anew.
That is the power of life,
For you.

Fall
by Brodie Cates

It is really cold.
Leaves are falling on the ground.
It is so awesome!

Friendship
by Elena Sofia Santini

Could you imagine being betrayed?
Getting a sinking feeling and feeling afraid.
Your face gets hot with anger,
Your heart begins to pound,
You begin to wonder if you can ever calm down.
The next day at school,
You act like you're cool.
Hiding feelings inside,
And you just want to cry.
The anger bubbles inside,
As you walk outside.
You hug your friend,
And the anger ends.
You walk back inside,
And the sadness dies.
I can always count on a friend,
To support me until the end.

Tiger of the Light
by Chrishton King

Tiger, tiger, in the light
Will it give you a great fright?
Will it flee or will it fight?
Will you cause it a great fright?
Will it show you all its might?
You might trust it in the day
But will you trust it in the night?
A wild tiger, it's not tame.
Will you choose it to blame
Will it attack in its graceful frame?
Which one of you has more of brain?
The tiger battles a knight in the night.
The tiger shows you all its might.
It will not flee, it will fight.

A Poem
by Uchenna Holder

My name is Uchenna, and I am awesome.
I am an awesome guy.
I am writing a poem.
An awesome poem, if you ask me.
I could be writing any poem.
But let's get it done.
Let's write a poem about hot dogs.
No, video games. No, candy.
How about we write what 1+1 is?
That's not even a poem!
Well, since I cannot decide, I won't write any poem.

Music
by Hannah Rison

So many notes in my life, so many songs in my soul
So many tunes in my heart, I can't keep control
Then you came in my life, I didn't know what to do
Every time I think about it, I know it's when I met you
You don't care how I look, you will still be my friend
Every time I see you, I know this friendship will never end
So many notes in my life, so many songs in my soul
So many tunes in my heart, I can't keep control

I Love Friendship
by Mone' Lawless

I love my friends.
We love to laugh and play all day.
We love to go outside even on a rainy day.
We run through the puddles without a care.
Even if we mess up our hair.
Happy, caring, and kind describes us.
With each other friendship is a must.
I love my friends.

Monarch Butterflies
by Maiya Leonard

Monarch butterflies are so elegant.
They fly through the sky but they're so delicate.
They are symmetrical which makes them look so fine.
They dazzle in the wonderful sunlight.
The stripes in their wings are their wonderful wing veins
Isn't that wonderful!
When I see them I feel so happy.

A Sister
by Avery Keown

From day one, I knew. I looked into her eyes so blue.
A sister's love, forever and always.
Her smile, her laugh, her first step and words.
A sister's happiness, beautiful and important.
I rock her to sleep, skin soft as a sheep.
She starts to cry, a tear falls from her eye.
A sister's care, fun and kind.
She learns to ride a bike, she loses a tooth.
It's like she grows up in a poof.
A sister's growth, amazing and magical
She starts 1st grade, I help her with homework.
A sister's education, big and endless.
She trips and falls, she cries and calls.
I'm there by her side, responsibility and pride.
A sister's health, crucial and serious.
We get into a fight, hurtful things were said.
Next day we apologize, a thing we siblings dread.
A sister's feelings, gentle and heavy.
We grow up together, arm in arm.
Sisters forever, even when I'm gone.

Something I Love To Do
by Shirley Edgerton

I am baking.
I am overjoyed.
I am making.
I am doing something I enjoy.
I am creating.

Basketball
by Peter Luster

You should play basketball,
because it is fun.
You play it with a hoop and a ball,
and play it in the sun.
I like basketball,
it keeps me in shape,
I run and jump,
but it's not for a primate.
Basketball is easy
Basketball is fun
Basketball is challenging
And it's for everyone!

America
by Scott Morrison

America has gone through thick and thin.
America is the perfect place to live in.
America has beautiful grassy hills.
America has millions of thrills.
Many climates all over.
Living in America is like finding a four leaf clover.
America has the best deserts.
Living in this beautiful country is like a huge dessert.
We have beautiful prairies.
Those prairies are very merry.
America has beautiful forests.
Some of those flowers can effloresce.
America has wonderful basins.
Those basins are worth chasing.
America's technology has advanced by far.
We even have electric cars.
America, America, my home sweet home.
America, America, I love my home.

The Run
by Noel Sterling

Have a ball in the hall,
with the best of best
I have more fun
when I run in the sun,
so run, run till the moon shines bright,
in the dark like a light
So rest your head in the bed,
and dream of the fun,
we had in the sun.

Much More Than Wind
by Faith Corbin

The spring breeze,
in the trees.
How peaceful and how pretty,
like birds flying in the city.
Causing the trees to sway,
in both night and in day.
It sounds so beautiful when it comes to mind,
when it leaves sorrow far behind.
Don't shut the window or you will lock it out,
filling your life with dreariness and doubt.
Because just feeling how it feels,
is like turning the feeling into wheels.
And reading this poem today,
will make you want to shout hurray.

Horrible Day
by Zharia Hill

Something's about this day.
I want to have it my way.
Entering school, as I walked in.
My horrible day now begins.
Kicked out of breakfast, for being too late.
But then I thought, "Why doesn't class just begin at eight?"
Made it to class.
In a quick flash
We started to test.
Makiya put paper on my desk.
I told her, "No!"
For that I got a zero.

Dedicated To All Veterans
by Sam Cox

Veterans have enlisted in the Army, Coast Guard, Air Force and Marines,
There's also the Navy, they sail in big submarines,
They all use very big and powerful machines.
The Armed Forces protect the country from sea to sea,
They let the American citizens live happily,
The Armed Forces let our country be free,
Veterans should be honored with glee.

Dark As Night But, Yet Still Shining
by Brock Winn

Dark as the night we hunt the streets.
Dark as the night we're scared as can be.
Dark as the night we're hard to find.
Dark as the night with sin we're blind.
Dark as the night we bleed from our scars.
Dark as the night it feels like there are bars.
Dark as the night we walk tall,
Dark as the night we give our all.
Dark as the night we create and discover.
Dark as the night we are different from all others.
In the night of this dark world you may not know who we are.
Rising from the dark we will stand out and shine like stars.
We may be dark as night but we are, yet still shining.

Weeping Willow
by Aylah Jordan

So many nights I've wept and I've cried, so many days have slipped by
Yet nothing has changed in the starry night sky,
Weeping Willow, let me stay with you, let your graceful arms embrace me
and hold me tight at night, let me drift away to a better place,
Weeping Willow, I say farewell to you, I've stayed here way too long,
it's time I go on home to the Promised Land
For once we might have laughed, once we might have cried
but now there's only silence as I have joined the sky
I'll watch you, Weeping Willow,
where I used to lie and cry with you time and time again,
but now I must leave you, Weeping Willow,
you must not weep no more
for farewell, Weeping Willow.

Fall
by Carter Saylor

Fall, spooky, scary,
Leaves all orange, yellow, red, brown,
Chilly, breezy, cool!

Mississippi Fishin'
by Halie Alford

I live in Mississippi where you find the Pearl River.
That's where I fish in my daddy's boat that's silver.
We unload the boat at Atwood in Mississippi.
It's a great place to drink Mello Yello
I can catch a lot of fish. With my homemade chicken liver dish.
You can find me with my fishin' pole. Off in the best fishin' hole.
My fishin' pole might be pink. But I can out fish you any day of the week.
We got the radio up loud. No worries even when there's a rain cloud.
Rain makes the magnolia. That's the state flower like I told ya.
We got the large mouth bass. Don't talk back 'cause we don't sass.
We like everything deep fried. Eat all your food, there's apple pie.
There's always pulled pork, no need for a fork.

My Pets
by Greta Whittington

My pets are grateful.
My pets are lovable.
One is very fat.
One is very skinny.
We call one fuzzy puppy.
They ride with me.
They sleep with me.
One of my pets went beyond the Rainbow Bridge.
One of them loves to eat.
One of them will be sad if she does not get treats.
My pets will eat anything.
One of them will run in the field.
One of them will run to the gate.
They will eat dirt.
They will eat all kinds of weird stuff.
They love to sit by the tree.
One loves to chase the chickens.
I love my pets.
Oh, how I love my pets.
All and all, I love them all.

Cat In the Hallway
by Chloe McMath

The cat in the hallway,
Has no owner.
There was a fire going, "BOOOOM"
The cat in the hallway called 911!
The firemen went there and sprayed out the fire,
The cat was saved!

Peace
by Liliana Gilbert

Once upon a time that hope and courage is rare, a girl found some in a flare ...
A little girl wondered if peace was real for slaves, for she was one,
that worked in the fields, was beaten of her shortness.
Her name is Mary; she fell asleep in a trance.
She dreamed of a star floating down to her, it said,
"You think peace is impossible, watch the future,
and you will gain hope and honesty and will thrive for this to go on."
"When you are older and away from war and injustice; tell of this!"
Mary saw a little girl like her, the future in a nice school learning,
Blacks and whites together with no conflict!
Mary was amazed what the future holds.
"What year is it, Star?" Mary asked. "2016, but this happens sooner.
Don't be shy when you go back, have hope and courage."
Mary found her peace in the world, will you?

Why?
by Nicole Sanfiel

Why? Why is a very good word. It tells how you're feeling.
Why? It says you're confused. It says you're worried.
Why? You can ask questions with the word "why."
Why is he Caucasian? Why is he African American?
And why are they not friends?
Why? Martin Luther King Jr. wrote a speech for us, the kids,
to hold hands as brothers and sisters.
Why? Just because I'm Spanish and you're white and she's black? Who cares?
Let's play and have a good time. But you say "No."
"Why?" I say, because she is white and I am Spanish.
Another word for this would be racism.
You say, "No, I just don't like you because you are not the same as me."
Why? As I said before, "why" is a very good word but sometimes it hurts.
Why?

Fire
by Terry Summers

Fire, a source of light
Burning so wild and very bright
Lighting up the night

My Brother
by Katelyn Hoffman

I love my brother in every way
he always makes my day
he makes me feel better when I am sad
he makes me feel better when I am mad
he is nice, unique and proud
he always makes me smile every day
Oh, I love him, yes I do
I couldn't replace him with someone new
I love the way he walks
I love the way he talks
I love the way he makes funny faces
Oh, I love him, yes I do

Heaven
by Kyle Chen

I look up at the ceiling
And then there's a bright flash.
The next thing I remember
The lights went out.
I opened my eyes
And saw a bright sun,
And there were rainbows all around
With clouds beneath my feet
I think to myself
Is this Heaven.
Then I find the answer
To my question.
There was a man
With wings as beautiful as gold
And with a smile
As warm as the sun.
I guess this is Heaven
Where I'll spend the rest of my life
In happiness
And peace.

I Am a Boy
by Ty Hoyt

I am a boy.
I am not special.
I am a kid.
I am not mean.
I am good and
I am nice.
I am a boy.

Lost At Sea
by Ra'Kiera Gibbs

We became lost at sea,
nobody knowing it was just us three.
Together we did what we could to survive,
but honestly we didn't think we would make it out alive.
Together we all went to great lengths,
doing all that we could using our strengths.
We found an island where we set up camp,
using all materials we could find to make an S.O.S. stamp.
Someone found us and saved the day,
now we know next time to never wander off at bay.

Water
by Jordan Cook

Water, such a beautiful thing!
Brings life and death to so many glamorous creatures.
It can be dirty or fresh and pure. Just like humans can be.
In so many places, all looks different.
Some dirty and brown and some blue and green.
So fresh, so pure. Keeps people alive. Puts dinner on the table.
Anything you need to keep yourself alive. Water.
Oh God, oh God brings water to our adoring, precious, beautiful lives
every day to keep us alive.
When I go to that glamorous, precious, magical kingdom
I will be the one who gives water to you!
People, so many people without water.
They suffer and have no way to survive. They can't bathe or stay clean.
Water is the most important thing in our precious, adoring lives.
Without water all of us would die.

Polar Ice Caps
by Caleb Figueroa-Carr

Polar ice caps
They are melting and we need to help them.
Stop using so much oil and gas.
Use more electrical stuff.
It is so sad to see them break off of the big group of ice.
Also a lot of animals are losing their homes and dying.
But if we stop heating the world with cars they will stay until the end of time.
Save the ice caps!

Funny Epitaphs
by Kaden Anderson

Here lies a runner by the name of Billy Cole
Was running on the road and died in a hole.
Here lies a news reporter by the name of Villager No. 9
Was reporting a war and was blown up by a mine.
Here lies an explorer by the name of Martin Hannibal
Was exploring in South America and was eaten by a cannibal
Here lies a clown by the name of Dax Brown
Was entertaining the town (yeah right, who likes clowns anyways)
And was left to drown.
Here lies a ghost hunter by the name of Martin Scary
Was ghost hunting and was too late to see Bloody Mary

My Voice
by Corinne Ginsberg

My voice comes from Boston, with long cold winters safe in my family's arms
And Brigham and Women's Hospital where doctors worked hard to keep me alive
From my mom and dad who loved me from the start
And from my sister Maddy who loved me from the moment we met
My voice comes from Grampy who I love and miss each day
From Aunt Katie who held me first, right after my parents
And from Grandma who gave me my musical talent
From Renee who took care of me when I was tiny and weak
My voice comes from my dance school where I happily dance each day
From my teachers, both dance and regular school
And from kindergarten where me and Julia became best friends
And now from fifth grade where I rule the school
My voice comes from my friends who I have loved since we met
From my cousins Evan and Cody who I love each and every day
From my dog Xana who loves to snuggle with me
And dances around every time I get home
And from Boston, with long cold winters safe in my family's arms.

My Weekend
by Zoya Khan

When I woke up in the morning
My brother was sort of boring
So, I went downstairs and felt bored
On my violin, I played a chord
I watched TV with my dad
But, then he got mad
I ran laps around the street with my sister
But, then I got a blister
Later, with my mom, I went to the store
When we came home, I went to bed
And started to snore!

Soccer
by Lyndon Porter

There are many different sports, but soccer is the greatest
It's better than football and it's the most edgiest
Soccer is my favorite sport, what more can I say
It's amazingly fun if you know how to run
Soccer is cool but it's also tiring
If you wanna give it a go, you have to push bro
Go, go, soccer, you are my favorite sport
I shall give it a must with all of my dust

I Am
by Nia-Simone Johnson

I am courageous and kind
I wonder about all the secrets of the world
I hear the sound of my alarm going off in my mind
I see the goodness of the Lord
I want to be one of the greatest people in mankind.
I am courageous and kind
I pretend to be Superman
I feel like I can fly
I touch the hearts of everyone
I worry about being shy
I cry when I feel sad and alone.
I am courageous and kind
I understand that I need to be nice to others
I say if you are kind to others, they will be kind to you
I dream of helping others
I try to be brave in everything I do
I hope that my future is great and divine.
I am courageous and kind

Ghost
by Aden New

Ghosts are cool and scary
they make you scream and shout.
They share the joy of having lots of fun each and every night.
They might scare you to death or make you laugh
but that is what they have to do for the rest of their never-ending life.
They love to meet you and have lots of fun
but it's sorry to say that they never can and never will
shake your very lucky hand.

Quarterbacks
by Trevor Emmert

So many people come from this position. It's just an NFL tradition.
People like Tom Brady, Peyton Manning, and many more.
I bet after games they're really sore.
Some quarterbacks are outright bad. After games the fans and the team are very sad.
My favorite is Tom Brady. Some people call him slow. Us Patriots call them foes.
People think Eli Manning is fire. When I watch him I get tired.
When the Patriots won 4 rings people say they cheating. They just mad we eating.

This Is My Soul
by Camden Malone

I am from unbearable heights with thick strands
I am from Georgia clay and a passionate family
I am from a background of bullying and hurt
I am from Indian jackets in ruins
I have felt the hand from the sky touch my heart every night
I am made of hot cocoa and marshmallows
I am from the one book of truth
I am from hikes to sitting in bed all day
I am from the southern girl on the corner street
I am from hot summer days to cold winter nights
I am from love at heart yet lots of fights
I am from Lulus biscuits and Popsicles galore
I am from Sunday dinners with old friends and more
I am from sorrow and death from closely loved ones
I am from one's faces lost in old memories
I am from a southern heart to northern charm
I am from Rocky Mountains and dentist's clowns
I am from high dives to ice waters
I am from zoo trips and smiley monkey faces
I am from close family and Jesus stays in mind

The A's
by Carson Reese Brown

My sister's name is Annielieese and that starts with A.
My cousin's name is Ashley, and that starts with A.
My mom's middle name is Arora and that starts with A.
Why so many A's
Why not my name with A

The Willow Tree
by Alexia Heck

The willow tree, it shall be where imagination sparks.
It's full of wonders as it shall seem, the willow tree is part of me.
Through the tree imagination flows, like a river of peace.
The tree speaks to me so clearly, and really makes me think.
Imagination, wonders, peace, speaks.
All of these make up me.

The Inspirational Sky
by Kendall Olson

In the sky, there are wonders I must try
To figure out why it speaks to me so clearly.
The clouds soar, the wind roars,
The rain falls, my love withdrawals.
There I feel peace, sparking right out of me,
I fly high with so much creativity in me.
I love the sky, and I know it will always be mine.

Who I Am ...
by Wyatt Hart

I am the chocolate cake to my face on my second birthday
and the dirt brown eyes from my father.
I am the heart of the dance floor.
I am the fighter of the flood when I was young.
I am the little girl who listened to my father say I might never see him again.
I am the hungry mouth to the grits and bacon
on the early Sunday mornings before church.
I am the cute little driver of the little pink car, and Barbie Jeep,
and the princess with the poodle skirt with a panda purse.
I am the arguer with my two little brothers,
but they are the peanut butter to my jelly.
This is who I am.

My Family
by Jena Murphy

There are many things in life that mean a lot to me,
but the most important will always be my family.
My family has always shown me lots of love
with endless kisses and endless hugs.
I have no doubt that my family will always be there for me
no matter what the issue may be.
I hope someday I will be able to take care of them
and show them the gratitude that I have within.
My family is truly a blessing to me,
how did God know they would make me so happy?
So my dear family, as I picture all of your faces,
I want to thank you for all your good graces.
Without each and every one of you,
my life would never be so happy and true!

Dreams
by Celeste Tatum

Dreams are wonders. What you think about in your sleep.
A land where wishes come true.
With play and fun, in your mind where anything is possible.
You dream and you dream, till your heart's content.
Not all dreams are good, no. You can have bad dreams too.
Bad dreams are filled with horror and fright,
sometimes you may shriek through the night.
When I think of something happy I dream about it all night.
When I see something scary I shiver in fright.
That's how I get nightmares.
Sometimes you might wake in the middle of the night.

Halloween
by Genesis Kennedy

Hello everybody, it's Halloween time again
Put on your costume, time to be seen
You can be a vampire or a ghost
A prince or a princess, or even toast
As we leave home and put on our shoes
Please remember the safety rules
Always go trick or treating with an adult
And never go into a stranger's house
Now is the time to knock on doors
And enjoy the lights and spooky decorations
When we knock on doors this is what we say
Trick or treat, smell my feet, give me something good to eat

Drums
by Will Bridges

The drums, go bang.
The birds, go squawk.
The trucks go past, in the city all night.
When the drums go bang.
Everything stops.
The carnival starts.
The rides, go 'round.
The fireworks go boom all night long.

The Sky
by Cameron Sutton

The sky is blue
when the weather is nice,
The sky looks high
when a jet passes by.
The sky is nice like a beautiful sight.
The sky is wonderful like my everyday life.
You can fly in the sky,
Like a butterfly,
You can see a plane in the sky,
Like a bird soaring high.

Sports
by Zachary O'Haver

Football, baseball, and basketball, I love them all.
Tennis, golf, and track, I love them to the moon and back.
Soccer, hockey, and lacrosse, all games where you toss.
Sports are fun and breathtaking. And they were all worth making.

A Picnic On the Lake
by Zaida Annan

The moonlight shines on the beautiful lake,
Classical music flowing through the air.
The taste of cheddar in my mouth,
So cheesy and fresh,
The lake glimmering in the night.
The crickets chirping under the trees,
The stars twinkling under the sky.
This is the greatness of the night,
The greatness of the moon.

The Happiness of Halloween Night
by Shriya Manikonda

The beautiful and colorful leaves everywhere on Halloween night
So inspiring and loving
Pumpkins everywhere, so nicely carved
Houses decorated in an extraordinary way
Seeing people going trick-or-treating
Halloween night is so pretty with the colorful season fall
Everyone is happy on Halloween night

Dreams
by Brianna Crow

They can be awful, or extremely awesome.
They can be exciting, or very uninteresting.
Good dreams,
Like getting all A's in school.
Or a bad dream,
Like failing an important test.
But sometimes, dreams can come true.
Others may disappoint you.
You'll never know.
That's the secret of dreams.

The Life Cycle
by Gigi Esposito

In a bright sunlight,
A planet we respect,
For God O'Mighty He made,
Jesus who saved,
The cross was held,
And never moved.
Wind blowing,
Nature's morning so beautiful.
Trees dropped seeds,
Rain weeped,
The earth made flowers,
Pond and land connected,
For fish, birds, and animals.
Colonies built in the free,
Always there in the night,
Broad moons, stars pass by.
By night, make a wish,
Keep it good,
So that it will come true.

Christopher Columbus
by Emily Lin

Long, long ago, in 1492
Columbus as we know sailed the ocean blue
He traveled on three ships and departed from Spain
Started on his trip, through sunshine and rain
There came days and days, the crew yearned for land
Patience went away, they dreamed of rock and sand
But ... oh wait! What do I see?
Is that an Indian? Next to that tree?
But "India" was not the land, Bahamas they had conquered
Though it was not as planned, the crew was honored

The Ball Fields
by Lily Qualls

I love the ball fields it's what I do, with all the people there it feels like a zoo.
The sounds I love are the crack of the bat and the smack of the glove.
The aroma of popcorn and pizza make my tummy rumble, sometimes I stumble;
but when I sit in the outfield getting all hot and sweaty
the smell of snacks gets me ready.
I hate the gnats and sun in my face,
but the red dirt tastes great when we come in first place.
The coaches are nice to meet, and they really like to compete.
At the end of the season we get the rewards
of trophies and friendships as we move forward.

What Is Orange?
by Jennifer Hock

Orange feels like a goldfish swimming in its tank
It is an orange crayon coloring a paper
Orange looks like an orange hanging on a tree
It is crackling fire laughing at me
Orange smells like cheddar cheese
It is a yummy tart waiting to be eaten
Orange tastes like orange Jell-O made just for me
It is a kitten looking at me
Orange sounds like a candy wrapper opening
It is the sun glowing on my face at the beach
Orange reminds me of pumpkins
It is the leaves beneath my feet

All You Can Eat
by Allon Ellis

I once went to a place that serves all you can eat
and how my new shoes do not fit my feet
my snap-back is too tiny to fit my head
my legs are now hung over my bed
so if you should visit- take my advice, brother
and don't stuff your face!

It's Special
by Milo Justice

This is the poem, the very special poem
don't ask me why, but I feel it, don't you? ...
It is special all day, it is special all night
can't you feel how special it is?
more special than an ocean, as special as life
I don't get why you don't think it's special
and no! It's not that I'm hungry, which I am
it's not that I'm tired, which I am
it's not even that I'm crazy, which I am
I really think it's special
I really really do
okay, I give up, I'm crazy, tired, and hungry too
you're right, I'm a loon.
Please don't tell, this special poem suits me so well!

Colors and Feelings
by Dylan Scott

I see the sky, the color is blue.
I see the road, the color is black.
I see the river, it makes me feel happy.
I see the car and I enter.
I see the colors. I feel the feelings.
I see white, it makes me talk about peace.
I see blue, it makes me feel like I am floating peacefully.
I think of purple, it makes me write.
I see the colors. I feel the feelings.
I see orange, it reminds me of mandarin oranges.
I see green, it reminds me of life.
I see brown, it reminds me of trees.
I see teal, it reminds me of my favorite color.
I see the colors. I feel the feelings.
I see grey, it reminds me of minerals.
I see red, it reminds me of apples.
I see the colors. I feel the feelings.

Love ... Hate ... Brothers
by Zeke Searcy

I am grumpy, I am mad
But sometimes, I am very glad.
Every day and every night
all I want to do is fight!
I am black! I am blue!
I am tired of fighting you!
You're my brother, let's pretend
that you are my very best friend.

Dream
by Jediah C. Mister

Dreams can be funny.
You enjoy them.
When you imagine them they help you know what you want to be in life.
Dreams tell you how it will be for you.
When you are a kid dreams will help you know what you want to be
when you grow up.
Dreams make you smile.

The Mysterious Man
by James Lackey

A man staring at the stars,
in the moonlight,
mysterious as can be.
Lying there, fascinated by the light,
shining down on the world.
Vanishing into,
the darkness of the sky.
Soaring past the moon,
light so bright,
like a flashlight.
Will he return,
or be trapped among the stars,
twinkling so bright,
under the moonlight?
Stars are to my left,
and to my right,
but their light is dimmed,
as the sun was rising,
upon the horizon.

What Bugs Me
by Emily Perricone

When I have homework
When my neighbor's dog barks
When my dog squeaks his toy
When my fridge beeps
When I lose my phone
When my sister takes my stuff
When we don't eat what I want
When I don't get my way
When it's time for math
When the O's lose a game
When I can't watch my shows
When I have to write a poem

A Mother's Love
by Elisha Howell

From an infant you named me, you held me,
you fed me, you rocked me, you bathed me,
you read to me, you loved me
From a toddler you "stop" me, you "no" me,
you "put that down" me, you "take that out" me,
you "good job" me, you loved me
Now that I'm older you support me, you comfort me,
you encourage me, you surprise me, you discipline me,
But you still love me

Moved Away
by Evelyn Pollitt

My life changed a lot
to go from Virginia to Maryland
to leave my best friend
to go to a new school
and to leave my neighborhood
all of my friends
and my teachers
I still see my friends
but not my teachers
we still hang out
but not as much
we used to be 3 houses away
but now we're an hour away
I miss my friends a lot
and some I won't see for a very long time.

Friends
by Mikayla Dykes

Fun
Reliable
In it to win
Exciting
Never-ending
Doesn't ever quit
Salvation.

Carbon
by Pranay Maini

About 20% of the weight of living organisms is carbon
More compounds are known which contain carbon than don't
Diamond is an excellent abrasive because it is the hardest common material
and it also has the highest thermal conductivity
One of the most important elements for all living things is carbon
Carbon can turn into diamonds over time
Carbon if pressurized underground over time it could turn into a mix diamond

Flowers
by Kenya Z. P. Walker

Flowers are fun because they are different colors.
Pink, purple, yellow and many others.
I like flowers because they are big.
I also like flowers because they are pretty.
Flowers are fun because they flop around.
I like them most because they can be picked from the ground.

What Makes Me Warm Inside?
by Taylor Winn

The sun makes me warm inside.
It glares on my face.
The beach makes me warm inside.
It's such a great, big, beautiful space.
My family's love makes me warm inside.
Because I know they love me so.
Hot chocolate makes me warm inside.
We drink it together when it is very, very cold.
All these things make me warm inside,
and I am glad of the wonderful things I feel and see.
The warm feeling inside makes me smile.
They all bring out the best in me.

Me
by John Makinde

John Makinde
Athletic, funny, strong
Lover of my family and dogs
Feels happy, bored
Who wonders what Heaven's gonna be like?
Who fears nothing yet,
Who cares about family and the poor.
Who is able to play sports.
Who dreams be president and time machine.

America's Trees
by Scott Funches, Jr.

When I wake up I see trees
All over the world people see
Trees bring life to nature
The animals and environment adore it
Listen closely and you can hear oxygen flow through the trees.
In the winter they're gone.
In the spring they bloom.
For summer it's hot.
In autumn they fall.
Enjoy trees and you will have a ball.

Butterflies
by April Beall

Butterflies
Drifting in the wind
Butterflies
Floating in the breeze
Butterflies
Spreading their wings with glee
Butterflies
Wings ready for flight
Butterflies
Such an amazing sight!

My Grandparents
by Jasmine Flowers

Jasmine
Friendly, kind
Learning, playing, talking
Soccer, granddaughter, grandmother, grandfather
Loving, traveling, helping
Generous, wise
Mommom and Poppop

Fun At the Park
by Gabriel Tolbert

On Monday it was a fun day,
because I went to the park with my friend Clark.
I knew I was going to have a fun day in the sun.
So I went out to play just yesterday.
But today I didn't play because I did that yesterday,
and yesterday is not today.

The World As I See It
by Aaliyah Vahora

If you ask me how I see the world, here's what I'd say.
The clouds I see look like cotton candy, the sea, it looks like me, why?
Because I see my reflection that's why!
Birds go fly when they go migrate but they don't say "hi" or "goodbye."
The grass is like one big fuzzy carpet that we're all standing on.
I might see the world differently than you but I see it the way I want it
but this is all in my imagination so I must have a big one!

The Beach
by Clare Ballweber

I feel the golden sand, in between my toes,
why the sand is golden, no one ever knows.
I taste the salty breeze, that blows upon my face,
whenever that wind blows, I'm in my happy place.
I wade in the majestic ocean, with sea creatures going by,
whenever a wave hits me, I feel like I can fly.
I observe the glorious sunset, the orange, pink, and red,
it feels right above me, right above my head.
This place is dear to me, it's held close to my heart,
well, most of the time, except when there's a shark!

Shield
by Jimmy Jones

Shields are used
Heavily for protection.
In hard times of battle.
Everyone someday may need a shield
Love and take care of your shield. The
Day may come that you will need it!

Me
by Gezzrelle Davis

Gezzrelle Davis
Smart, small, quiet
Lover of fish, shopping, dance, fam
Who feels bored
Who wonders where animals go when they die
Who fears elevators
Who cares about fam
Who dreams of being a teacher
Who is able to swim

The War
by Emily Okerblom and Alyssa Fleming

She's fighting a war,
And so am I,
I often like to ask my mother why,
Do we go here or do we go there,
All of this began with a scare,
She doesn't like the chemo,
But I sit here believing though,
That she will make it another day,
We pass through the graveyard,
It is just me and my sister now,
We live on the street,
And we don't have much to eat,
Because we walk around on our bare feet,
A year later,
Things have changed,
The war goes on,
And things are still strange,
My life story is not to be scared or afraid,
But to continue without fear,
And be ready for change.

Bunny and Kitty
by Anna Oviatt and Mia Szirovecz

A bunny met a cat and started to bat but then the cat sat on a mat
and took away the bat so the bunny said, "Then you sat on my mat!"
So the cat started to pat the bunny's hat.
The bunny grabbed the hat and the cat sat on the mat.
Then the bat flew in and sat on the cat.
The cat got mad and the bunny got sad.
So all of them ran into the hall and started to fall.
Then the cat started to scream, and the bat called her mean.
The owner said "HEY! Don't scream!"
The cat stopped screaming and the bat stopped talking.
The whole house was silent.
Then they all left the room, and the bat grabbed a broom!
And began to try to fly to the moon! "What a silly cat!" said bat.
Cat thought it was bunny, and cat grabbed bunny's tail; and bunny began to squeal!
Owner got mad so away he sent the cat!
The cat sat on the red mat in time-out.
The cat began to cry. Bunny ran over to the cat and became her BFF!

This Is My Story ...
by Caroline Scharff

I am from a crackling firepit on cold autumn days making leaf piles with brothers.
I am from the Lord's Prayer reciting every dark night
while *Goodnight Moon* traded off by Mom and Dad.
I am from family vacations with burning jellyfish stings
but playing in the ocean and tubing on waves.
I am from a family that always wants to win,
but cheers on everyone no matter what.
I am from family picnics at the park as a little girl,
digging up red Georgia clay on my feet as I run.
I am a pinch of dimples every time the camera flashes.
The feel of fresh, cold water diving in for a swim meet.
I am from two older brothers playing Monopoly all Christmas Eve.
Sitting in bed on early mornings, learning my ABC's.
I am from eating messy ribs, every birthday dinner.
Seeing the smile on my face, as I'm eyeing the cake.
I am from long days of swim practice, after a very tiring day.
Flashbacking the fun times spent with my friends as I rest from a day of play.
This is my story and this is all about me,
I love my life as a kid and just being unique.

Soldier
by Charles Belflower

Someone who protects us, and is trained to fight for
Our country and destroy enemies to protect. They
Light our souls with happiness and we cheer them on. They
Drive tanks, trucks and airplanes, too. They fight and come back
In victory! We should pray for them and hope they win to
End enemies with guns and military vehicles, too. They try to
Reinforce other teammates, so they are not overwhelmed!

Man's Best Friends
by Anthony Chambers

Dogs are strong.
They run in the grass while holding a bone.
Dogs are big.
So that means they can dig.
Dogs are fast.
They are a blast.
Dogs are the best.
Teach him not to make a mess.

Mrs. Sunny
by Katelyn Johnson

Mrs. Sunny likes to sing her favorite song.
No matter what she's doing, she sings it all day long!
She sings it at a dance.
She sings it like she's in a trance.
She sings it in tubs.
She even sings it while she scrubs.
She sings it at all times.
She sings it even while she rhymes.
She sings it to a jar.
She sings it in the car.
She sings it when she pays.
Even on her birthdays!
Will she just be, she even sings it to me!
The only time she quit was when she was hit.
But she still remembered the song!
She knew it all along!
Her favorite song is "Shake it Up,"
But when she sings it, I think she should break it up!

Nature
by Ryanna Bucklew

Close your eyes, imagine that you are in a forest next to the top of a waterfall.
It is night, owls are flying by.
You look at the waterfall, you notice that it is glowing,
this is because the stars are shining down on you and the world.
A cool wind blows by.
Trees are swaying, crickets are chirping,
and a baby wolf and its parents come up to you.
You befriend them.
You start to get tired.
Lying on the grass, the wolves come and snuggle with you.
You slowly close your eyes while you look up at the beautiful sky.
You can open your eyes now.
Think about what you saw.

In the Autumn ...
by Layne Metzler

In the autumn I see big SUVs.
In the autumn I hear leaf blowers
In the autumn I taste angel cake.
In the autumn I smell fall breezes
In the autumn I feel chilly breezes.

Hopeless Night
by Nila Joseph

I look around the dark, hopeless night
Feel like I can't do anything right
It seems to go on forever
When will it end, it looks like never
My heart keeps on beating fast
Don't know how long I might last
But I won't let fear put me down
Gonna stand tall and put my foot on the ground
I look up into the twilight
Just ignoring all my fright
I turn my frown
Upside down
And suddenly I see the light
Like a flame in the sky
See the darkness fly away
Time to start a new day
The clouds, no longer grey
And I am glad to say
That the hopeless night has gone away

Talayla Kieper

Sister's Song
by Talayla Kieper

Through the glass I see you,
Such tiny little hands.
I cannot reach to touch you,
For this I was banned.
Mommy says they make you sleep a lot,
In order to get strong.
Your little lungs do not work,
So to you I sing this song.
"Rest little brother,
Don't you make a peep.
I want you to get better,
So please get your sleep.
I'll stand by your side,
In the day or night.
Whispering soft songs,
So you will not be fright.
When your eyes open up,
You will finally see.
Your big sister waiting,
To give you your teddy."

Siena Lee

Blaze
by Siena Lee

Heatedly dancing up and down,
Its orange light flickering up and over the shadows.
Pushing away darkness with a soft yet fierce glow,
Warmth flowing from its twirling flames.
Gray clouds puff up from its irritated crackling.
It burns down, extinguishing to become embers …
Only remnants of its once harsh temper.

1st Place

Camille Ollard

Camille is a bright young author,
currently in the 5th grade,
who not only enjoys writing, but playing the piano as well.
Gymnastics is also one of her favorite activities.
Keep up the good work, Camille!

My Pencil Is a Dancer
by Camille Ollard

She dances
twirling and swirling,
across the milk white paper,
her stage.
To me, a sentence.
To her, a dance
twirling, swirling, circling, flowing
with the music.
Scratch, scratch,
the sound of her bright red shoes.
Her flowing dress
like a bloomed daffodil.
At the end of every dance
she takes one last step
leaving behind one small dot.
She pauses
then floats up to join her fellow dancers
wearing identical yellow dresses.
Exhausted,
ready to view the next show.

Division II

Grades
6-7

Fire - Ice
by Toni Rogers

Fire
Hot, dangerous
Flaming, burning, mesmerizing
Flames, embers, snow, winter
Freezing, glistening, melting
Cold, beautiful
Ice

School
by Marie Gill

I don't like to do work
I like the nice teachers
I don't like carrying heavy books
I am scared of taking tests
I don't like doing homework
I love to go to recess and lunch

She Had My World
by Ella Sanders

She held the world upon a string
But she didn't ever hold me
If only someone would tell her how much she meant to me
But who could love me, I am out of my mind
She was like throwing a line out to sea
She made herself so hard to find
But it sure didn't ruin her, it just made her more interesting
When I looked into her eyes I saw the sky
The sun was always in her eyes, she didn't ever notice me
But who could love me, I am out of my mind
She was more than a prize
Why was I so blind and unrefined
What if she realized I did love her
Learning comes with its smiles and frowns
It just happened to be one of my downs,
It just happened that I wasn't in her world,
It just happened that she was only in my world
She was my creation, my imagination,
but she was still beautiful to me
-Inspired by Panic! At the Disco, "She Had the World"

My Shoe
by Timmani Jolley

Once there was a shoe, not just any shoe,
a shoe that was nice, that you kiss it goodnight until your lips turn blue
a shoe that you always shout, "I love you"
a shoe, a shoe, a shoe that if it took something you would have no clue
a shoe, not just any shoe, not pants, a dress or slippers, it's a shoe
a shoe, a shoe, it could be for me or for you, a shoe, a shoe, a shoe

The Winning Shot
by Sultan Seales

It is the 4th quarter, my heart is pounding,
pounding so hard you can hear the sounding
One basket to make, one win to take
Thinking what all would happen if I make this shot,
man, I would be one lucky pot
I shoot, I score
all my friends come at me with galore,
a galore of love, that is what is flying above
That what was what I wanted since I was a little nub,
I'm glad it wasn't taken away, that was so that game
I would think to play, but today we will all say HOORAY
That is when I knew everything was ok.

Love
by Gabrielle Fedrick

love, what a beautiful thing
love sustains an old figure
and blossoms anew
it can feel like you flew
so what is this feeling
it is so intriguing
yet it is always there
love can lead to a broken heart
from the strife of casualty
love, such a beautiful thing
but yet it is so incomprehensible
love leaves a warm feeling in its wake
love it is a bright and airy feeling
so why do we conceal it
it is meant to be shared
love, what a beautiful thing

Autumn
by Anna Pasquarelli

Autumn, a painter, a dancer, a mother
Painting leaves pumpkin orange, gold and brown
Dancing and whirling and swirling and leaping
Gathering leafy children and tossing them 'round
Laughing, they giggle, tumbling to her arms
Tossing tiny colorful acrobatics.

Halloween Night
by Brooke Sears

Doorbell ringing
Lights are blinking
Trick-or-treating door to door
Darker and darker outside it gets
More candy, more candy
kids cry like a witch
Halloween is scary
but some people are brave
At some doors they shout, boo-hoo
But we won't be afraid

Harriet Tubman
by Julien Berman

Sweet chariot
Comin' over yonder
"Every great dream begins with the dreamer," said she
This train
A conductor – metaphorically underground
A line without tracks
A thousand men smeared in tar, colored
Then freed by her hand
By our chariot
Stridin' across the ridge
She brought a gift
Security she called it
To me, she was the winged chariot more like
She flew, never got caught
She brought us away, to this security thing
We never knew what security was
In "security"
Covered in tar or not
We lived in peace
All because of one goddess

Good Times
by Lara Castillo

You know it now, you knew it then
This is the end of your line
You want to cry but you can't
'Cause this is the end of your line
So close your eyes and lie down
And think about your life
Remember the time when you fell for the girl
That turned out to become your wife
Remember the time when your daughters fought
And the little one took the blame
Remember the time when you got mad
It turned out to be a mistake
Remember the times you got sick
Your daughters did what they could
And there you are where the angels sing
And then you remember the time when your older one died
And you felt very sad
And you made your way to the highest cloud to see her shining bright
You never want to leave this place again
'Cause this is where you belong.

The Land of Wonder
by Sara Blades

They say the sky's the limit but what if there's more than that?
What if there's another place where people hang their hats?
Past Earth, past Mars, past all the other planets too
There might be another place and you never even knew
They might have people, they might have aliens
They might have made up words like "squalien"
They might say goodbye to say hello
They might have some things that make you say "whoa"
This place might have things we've never even thought up
This place might have something like the never-ending cup
This place might do something other than school
This place might think that really weird things are cool
The place that I think of might have a ruler of the land
They could possibly make their own rules and walk hand in hand
Maybe their land is ruled by mules
Or they could even have no rules!
So even if this place seems pretty weird
And if to you this place is feared
Or even if it seems like a zoo
Just remember that it might be the place for me and for you!

Sunken Flying Ship
by Mason Head

The new forgotten mystery
That's worth more than a dime
It's now lost in history
And now sung in rhyme
The unsolved riddle
Of how all were deceived
Now all people twiddle
On how they wished answers were received
The questions remain
On why the ship sunk
The loss of all in vain
Lost deep under the junk
The ship once held
What is no more
That once made people compelled
And left them all sore
The first flying ship
Lost unto sea
Not one has found even a blip
On how it lost its free

My Mind's Anxiety
by Rachel Rao

My mind's anxiety gets the best of me
I can't do what I want, a free life? I can't see
With every small thing, thoughts surround my head
"You're doing it wrong!" My mind's voice says
"Why are you holding me back?" I say to my mind
I feel so worked up, can't relax or unwind
"I'm just pressuring you not to mess up," my mind replies back
Giving a huff, "Please stop doing that!" I snap at my mind
"It gives me such fear. Just say something kind!"
"Oh alright I'll try," my mind answers again,
"Rating you, you're a five out of ten."
"That wasn't nice!" I exclaim to my mind.
Now, my self-confidence doesn't seem quite as high
"You just don't get it," my mind explains back
"If we worked together, we'd be back on track."
"So what must I do?" I inquire of my mind
My mind reviews, "Our thoughts must be redesigned."
"You need to think positive and happily, take a stress cleanse."
I nod and agree. But now as I go on, I'm beginning to see
The only thing holding me back is me.

The Journey
by Melissa Mazuranic

She looks for herself
In the maze
Scared of all the twists and turns
But the journey is hard
She knows it in her heart
Because she can't start the next chapter
Without reading the rest of the page

Winter
by Lexi Fountain

The falling snow
The crunch of the thick ice
The sweet taste of snow cream
The children playing, screaming, having snowball fights
Snow, who doesn't love snow
The cold, oh the cold
Mittens, coats, snowsuits, everyone's freezing
Everyone's shaking trying to get a little heat.
Guys giving their sweatshirts to their girlfriends
Oh what a wonderful time

The War Within
by Sara Gaddis

The war of great pain,
The one with no gain.
Fighting year after year,
I only feel fear.
Deep down inside
We crumble and hide.
Our army advances with courage,
The others discouraged.
Our one goal is to win
This battle within.
Our army, their army,
We fight till we're through,
The others tell you.
You've been fighting for years.
You've only felt fear.
Their army, retreated,
My enemy, defeated.
All that remains is the conflict inside.
Who you've been fighting for years, who can no longer hide.

Trinity
by Trinity James

I am an amiable person.
I'll always try to make several friends.
I don't talk rudely about people at all.
I help my classmates/friends if they need help.
I respect my classmates and they respect me.
I am Trinity Denise James.
And this is me.

Life As a Kid
by Donnisha Smith

Life as a kid is amazing
riding your bike with your friends,
you may fall on a log but,
Life as a kid is amazing
Life as a kid is hard
going to school getting those A's are rocky but,
Life as a kid is hard
Life as a kid is adventurous
trying new things in life
like a fear of heights
Life as a kid is adventurous

Hope
by Emily Perullo

It is ok to feel sorrow,
For everyone has felt it once.
It is ok to struggle,
When you feel good times are in the past.
It is the cloud around everyone that shines,
That leaves the enemies scrambling into fear of right.
This is just an act of violence,
That leaves everyone in awe.
It's time for this world,
To rise above.
Let the nation spread hope and love,
For it is good to fight for each other than against.
Be light in a world of darkness,
For hope will rise again.
Hope will be the voice for the mute,
The sound for the deaf.
Sing out to everyone you know,
Hope will rise again.

Love Is
by Alayna McCullough

Love is like an anchor buried deep in the soul
the thing that makes you crazy and makes you lose control
Love is like a river, flowing smooth and steady
Love is like a river, you're not going to be ready
Love is like a flower, blooming one day
dying the next, then going away
Love is like the moon, high up in the sky
above all the stars, and hoping it never dies
Love is a dream, deep into the night
Wishing it was real, tucked in tight

Nature and an Inside Creation
by Bailey Witt

Grass is green, weeds are green.
The sky is blue, flowers are blue.
Bugs are red, books are read.
Dogs are black, blocks are black.
The clouds are white and air is white.
I am a sister, you are a mister.
I am a brother, you are a mother.
Oils are smelly and bulls are smelly.
Clocks are white, blocks are white.
The night is black and the sky is bright.
Vegetables are tomatoes, vegetables are potatoes.
Better is water is better.
Tissues are issues are tissues.

Untitled
by J'nae Player

When I see his face I blush, but when he sees me I turn away in a rush.
He talks to me, with eyes sweet in a good way,
but me myself too shy, I have nothing to say.
If I could I would talk to him, oh our words would meet,
if only that could happen, I could barely stand on my feet.
If only he was in my class, we would have a blast,
but I'm scared he wouldn't think I'm cool, way too fast.
I keep my head up high and leave it to the past.
When I stare into his droopy eyes it makes me want to cry.
I try to impress but me, to less he will never address.
I think about him in my dreams at night but in the morning it goes away in a sight.
I gossip about him twice a day in the hallways at gaze.
One day just one, we will reconcile together in a happy sight.

Karate
by Alejandro Garduño

One kick you're down,
Two kick break it down
One punch, two punch, three punch, four.
If you move slow just go with the flow.
One chop, cut it down,
Two chop, chop it down.
Take karate or you'll be sorry.

The Chaos of My Heart
by Rebecca Holland

Tears fill my eyes
Like a river
Or stream flowing through me.
Blood thickening as it beats like acid rain on my face,
Wondering how it's possible.
Waterfalls of love fill my chest
But God will fill it when it's hollow.
The salty ocean rises along with my feelings and washes away all the pain.
Clips of unheard laughter whistling through the wind
as sand tornadoes take flight to the clouds.
Then I go back to reality
Where I'm relieved that my heart's still ... beating.

Swirl
by Maya Burton

I am surrounded by words I do not know the meaning of,
By laughter, when there is nothing amusing
By emotions I cannot identify and yet
I am surrounded by love and kisses
By laughter ringing with meaning
By words sung loud and clear
Words I understand
Things swirl around me from objects to actions
I am stuck in a whirlwind of things
I am surrounded by intelligent conversations and ideas
By justified happiness, by people who won battles, and yet
I am surrounded by unreasonable tears
By ideas and conversations not worth
Being had
By people with battle scars on the losing side
But being aware, possessing that knowledge
Is enough to set me free

The Lights
by Carey Bailey

Outside I am out on the street
Might find a new friend I want to meet
Running, playing, having lots of fun
The seeker finds me, I gotta run
Playing every sport we can all day
Till it turns dark I can say what I say
I mostly like playing b-ball games
On my friend's court call me LeBron James
Crossover, run, jump and dunk
I think today I might hide in my trunk
All fun and games is always right
To play until dark when it turns night
The sun is setting to make this night
The problem is I see the lights
The lights, the lights, the lights, oh no
"Sorry guys, I gotta go!"
I see my friends wave goodbye
Will I get home, I guess I will try
Running and running, feeling kinda sad
That when the lights come on I see my dad

Sirens, Family, and Hope
by Ariel Greenway

I know what is coming
It's the middle of the night
Ambulances and sadness
Just thinking about it gives me a fright
I know what is going to happen
As the people haul her away
I really wish my sister could stay
When I try to sleep
It's hard because the memory of that moment is so deep
At 3:30 I lie awake, the reasons are hard to say
The next day it's harder
For me to get a jump starter
On that day but what comes to mind
Is that everything heals with time
I can't stay sad or I'll never go farther
The more time passes by with me
My attitude goes back to being smiley
Even though this isn't the first time it has happened
Each time someone comes back, the more sadness begins to lack within
As hope, happiness, and love build in me

The Running Water
by Elijah Heald

The running water
By the trees and rocks it flies
Snaking through thy hills.

Life Is Like
by Jada Montford

Life is like
A glass bottle,
So fragile and wonderful,
And filled with many adventures.
Life is like
A gigantic painting,
So big and majestic,
And filled with many memories.
Life is like
A giant black hole,
So mysterious and never-ending,
And filled with many deep, dark emotions.
Life is like
A box of chocolates,
So sweet and delicious,
And filled with love and joy.

Friendship
by Lindsey Malcolm

Friends are like your safety net,
Treat them well and they will catch you.
Your friends will always be there,
Just like your safety net will too.
Wherever you go, your friends will have your back,
Whenever you fall, your net will catch you.
Your friends are your safety net,
And you are theirs.
Friends will always be there for you,
As you should be there for them.
Friendship will never be a one-way street,
It's an intersection
Where all friends have each other's back.
Ships will sail and sink,
But friendships will stay afloat
As long as a friend will mend any cracks.
Your friends are your safety net.

The Watery World
by Lana Adams

I swim deep beneath the surface of the earth in the deep blue.
I see exotic fish and dramatic coral covering the ocean floor.
I see the light shine on the water creating a pattern too,
It's like another world behind a different door.
Oh the watery world!
I look above and below me, and what do I see?!
A great white shark; I watch him lurking in the dark.
He is hunting for food.
He swims up toward me, and he pokes me with his rough, scaly snout.
Luckily, he does not engage; I am safe!
Oh the watery world!

What I Would Like To See
by Katie Mitchell

What I would like to see is world peace, everyone getting along.
What I would like to see is nobody getting judged for who they are.
What I would like to see are good leaders,
people who know how to help when others are in need.
What I would like to see are no more deaths from violence.
What I would like to see is nobody being afraid
to go out of their house because of others.
What I would like to see is everyone getting a voice, everyone gets heard.
What I would like to see is equal pay for equal jobs.
What I would like to see is education for everyone.
What I would like to see is so much more than this,
why don't we try and make it happen?
What would you like to see?

Life
by Ayden Wescott

Down from Heaven comes a little soul
Who does not know the journey that is about to unfold
Its puzzled eyes look around, wondering what things surround
Now he has started to walk and with that comes the gibberish he talks
Now a little lad you see, just started school last week
Now comes the tragic years, where the young boy disappears
And now becomes a teen, so intolerable and so mean
Now comes the young adult you see, he got his driver's license and ID
Now comes the day when the wedding bell rings
And you cannot seem to stop crying
Now he is an old grandpa and goes by the name Papa
And now nearing his end, he does not care because there is still Heaven

The Angel For Me
by Kay'La Brennon

As I sit and stare up at the sky
I look into the heavens and these words make mercy
God send me an angel so sit with me today
An angel that would wipe all my tears away
An angel that would encourage me each and every day
An angel that would stand by my side, be faithful and true
An angel that would never leave me with what I'm going through
God send me my own personal angel, one that reflects you
An angel that could say to me today is your day
You need not to think, worry, fret, or fear
Leave all that to me that's why I'm here
An angel who would let me lay and rest while they deal with the stress
How wonderful that would be, an angel that's all mine, if you would
An angel all to myself, if I only could
Oh I prayed and prayed until my God replied
He said that the only angel you want is the one you need
An angel to love and be by your side, an angel to be your guide
I understand what angel I very much need
The only angel I need is God himself

Don't Add Anything About How Beautiful You Are
by Jadaijah Hudson

Don't try to add anything that's not you to yourself
Because you're already beautiful the way you are
I'm not beautiful like you
I'm beautiful like me
Be your own kind of beautiful.
Always remember you're gorgeous
Don't let anybody tell you otherwise
What you think of yourself is much more important
Than what anybody thinks of you.
We get so worried about being pretty
Let's be pretty kind, pretty funny
Pretty smart, pretty strong
No matter how plain of a woman you may be,
If true and honest are written across her face
She will be beautiful.
Being called pretty or beautiful
Is so much nicer than being called hot or fit
Being nice makes you beautiful
Beauty isn't makeup.
Confidence is beautiful no matter your size
No matter your skin tone
Be confident in who you are and you will be beautiful.

Green
by Elijah Colie

Green is the color of nature.
Green is the sound of beautiful birds chirping in a field.
Green is the scent of pretty flowers in the spring.
Green is the taste of delicious lima beans.
Green is the feeling of getting a lot of money.
Green is the feeling of your best day ever.
Green is the feeling of eating homemade ice cream.
Green is the taste of Mountain Dew.
Green is the feeling of holding a Shih Tzu.
And green is a color that is beautiful and alive.

The Boy and the Beautiful Nature
by Kylie Allen

Once there was a boy who loved nature
He had joy in watching the animals speak,
flowers grow like trees and nature bigger and bigger
In his eyes the trees were taller than towers and butterflies as bright as gold on a ring
The sky was as bright as the sea and the grass as green as could be
The birds sang songs as sweet as honey to a bee
The stars sparkled like diamonds in the sky
When the boy closed his eyes he could fly as high as a bird in the sky,
when he closed his eyes
And went high in the sky he could be anything he wanted to be
To him the beauty of nature was as magnificent as could be

Water, Fire, Air, Earth
by Abriella Cortes

Water flows, fire glows,
Air blows, as the earth grows.
The ocean is blue, and fire is red, orange, and yellow true,
As wind whispers to the trees,
And the earth sits there giggling at the news with the trees.
Water is wet, fire burns,
Air plays in the sky, and the earth yearns to know why.
The seasons go by.
Water turns to ice, then it melts,
Fire is put out and then starts again,
Air makes haste while it snows,
And the earth just sits there and waits.
But then something happens.
The earth hears giggling, laughing, playing, it's coming louder and harder,
Because people love fire, earth, air, and water!

The Truth
by Jahdya Antoine

I'm not lazy, I'm a leader.
I'm not dependent, I'm independent.
I'm not ghetto, I'm glorious.
I don't have attitude, I have personality.
I'm not stupid, I'm sophisticated.
I'm not just another girl, I'm a beautiful young black woman!

Believe
by Amanda Raimondo

Believing, believing is simple,
not like trying not to giggle
but simple - it's not a mess,
it's not to impress.
Well, sometimes but it's more than this.
You, you have to be
true to you, to just pull through
but also, to believe in your success
to be the best of the best
to give no less.
So I'll believe in myself
And I'll put my trophy on my shelf.

I Can Be Cool
by Kimmiaya Hudson

I can be cool
And I can be cruel
I might be shy
But I can be the sky
If I cry
I can't be fly
I maybe hurt
But I'm not dirt
I love God
But people are not odd
My hair can be brown
But I got me a crown
We shall not be called trash
But if I do my all
I can say I got cash
I may be cool
Don't mean I'm a fool
And girl's rule

Money
by Russell Johnson

Money makes people greedy
Thankfully I'm not that needy
Money can buy almost anything
Except salvation with God we sing
But I prefer petting a bunny
Instead of getting all that money
Friends and family are all I needy
Money just makes people greedy

Rainbows
by Morgan Boyett

Red, orange, yellow, green, blue, violet.
When it rains a rainbow comes by to say hello.
It's there to brighten your day up.
I can't believe God put it in the sky.
It is amazing.
It shines like a star and it is so colorful.
It helps me think of my future and what is ahead of me.
It also can help you get through your day.
That is why rainbows are amazing.

The Fall of the Ring
by Zackary Glauser

The winds blow gently across the land
as all the heroes seem to stand
Against the king but many have no talent
they just seek the ring that falls all men
But one day the king was beaten
but the ring was found by a cretin
Named Gollum, but the ring
was stolen, not by a golem
But by a hobbit small named Bilbo
and gave it to his son
To try to beat the riders in the shawls.
His son, Frodo was sent on a quest
to ensure what none could best to hasten ...
the fall of the ring.
The fall of the ring.
Little Frodo Small was sent to destroy the ring
To prevent darkness
Restore the light.
-Based on "The Lord of the Rings" and "The Hobbit" by J.R.R. Tolkien

Stay Calm
by Nana Akuffo

Here we go, another day
school is here, no time to play
wake up early, with no light in sight
but think of dreams of no fright but flight
You are now at school thinking about your test
Now you are very stressed
You think, if I get an A, I have been blessed
in the classroom lies a paper
You think, I should leave and take it later
You know you can't leave, you must stay
You have to think, no time to play
you get your results, you open your mouth in awe
you took your test without a flaw

Pompeii
by Gabriella Ganoe

It started as a normal day
Everyone carrying out their daily duties
We thought nothing of it when Vesuvius started smoking
But then, the ground started to shake and quiver
And suddenly day turns to night
The heavens rain down ash and pumice
Women and children screamed
Dogs barked and whined
People searched and cried for their families
Thousand of people stampeded towards the river
Some did not make it
The ash buried them alive
Frozen in their poses
Our fair city, Pompeii, is buried

Who Am I
by David Knott

My name is David, it starts with a D, I run all around and people like me
My favorite subject is math, not to mention I take long baths
I don't like to play with toys because I am a big boy
I like reading and science too, but liking math is what I do
My favorite color is red, some people say I have a big head
I know that I'm smart and I'm ok at darts
I like to have fun under the bright yellow sun
I am caring and right now I am sharing
My name is David, it starts with a D, and I am glad that I am me

Distance
by Joelle Hayden

Distance can mean many things, it can be short, long, or even right in front of you.
What distance means to me is being separated from someone you love.
To be exact, it's 1,365 miles away.
I haven't seen you in over a month and I miss you terribly.
I know you're having fun at school and cheering at football games
but I hope you know I still miss you.
Since I left, you have been saying the same thing,
"Don't dream the reunion; plan it" and that's exactly what I'm going to do
and maybe one day we could break the distance and see each other again.
Hopefully I see you soon. See you later, "Bestfran."

Change
by Abigail Morman

You may think things stay static.
Never really changing.
But truthfully, that's not the case.
Things are changing, as you are reading this.
When you finish this poem, many things may have come in, and out of the world.
Though it may be hard to think about,
Just know that there are 8 billion other people on this Earth beside you.
Some you may not meet, and some you may not greet, but they are still there.
Never leaving till their time is right.
The world is changing, not asking for permission.
To change.

Never Give Up On Accomplishing Your Goals
by Eiza Yousif

Goals are the plan for our dreams, they are the dreams we want to catch
We should never give up on them and we should always chase them till the end
Accomplishing a goal is a stepping stone in life
Each time we accomplish a goal we become a different person
Goals are our wishes we hope to accomplish
They are our motivation and our light in the dark
Goals keep us going
Life without goals is a bird without wings
Goals are truly like magnets, the things that attract goals always come true
Keep your goals out of your reach
Set your standards high but don't keep your goals out of sight
Instead of thinking about luxury and working, give time to your family and friends
Spend time accomplishing your hopes and dreams and your goals
Goals are the plan for our dreams, they are the dreams we want to catch
We should never give up on them and we should always chase them till the end

Messi Mess
by Carmello George Barnett

Messi is very messy
He never cleans his mess
And he always takes his desk
He is the best in his league
He always needs a lead
And he loves eating peas

Mom
by Katarynna Pizarro

She holds me in her arms so tight
She comforts me in the dark of night
She pays for me to play sports and go to school
She gently places a blanket over me when the weather is cool
She is so funny and smart
I love her with all my heart
So I pour my heart into her hands
She really understands
She always wipes my tears away
She makes me smile every day
The love that we share is so strong
I know from her actions and the words of her song
I love my mom
She is the bomb

Sometimes
by Mykala Bledsoe

Sometimes in this world, I feel like an ocean
My emotions spread out like sea shells on the sandy shore
Treacherous trenches unknown
Carrying undesirable creatures in the depths of my mind
Some days I feel like a book with 1000 pages
Words and thoughts as abundant as ivy in an untamed yard
A plot line that cannot be foreseen or expected
Only those who are patient enough will understand my story
Other days I feel like a thunderstorm,
People watching from afar, afraid to get too close
Walls of grey blocking my view
With no idea how to contain the lightning growing inside me
Most days I feel like a pocket
Containing items of another person's belongings
Serving a purpose that goes unnoticed
Stuffed until I tear apart, leaving the items sprawled out for all to see

Succeed
by Kyree Blick

Succeed, achievement, and successfulness
What's going to get you money in life

Tears
by Olivia Stann

Tears of sadness, wish me away
Wish me a place where I may stay
Tears of sadness, make me a home
Make me a home without wood, without stone
Tears of sadness, make me a home
Make me a home where love may roam
For love is the base of many a heart
So give me a place where love can start
For without love, there are pits of despair
Only for those without love, without care
Tears of sadness, roll out of my eyes
Only for you do tonight I cry
Tears of sadness, save me from hate
Save me from those in that wretched state
Let me rise up, up into the sky
So that forever, tears of joy I may cry

My Family Is My World
by Brian A. Rolle, Jr.

My family means the world to me,
They forever and always will be,
I love them unconditionally,
And I receive their love for free.
I don't love them because of what I can get,
Because their love rewards me bit by bit.
Just their presence makes me feel so warm inside,
I would, nor could, find a greater love even if I tried.
Whether we are at home, watching movies or playing games,
I enjoy having fun with my family even it may seem lame.
Or if we are going out to eat or shopping,
This family here does everything.
Of course we fuss and argue like any normal family,
But we use forgiveness and resolve our problems peacefully. (Most of the time.)
We love and respect each other,
And we are grateful to have one another.
That is why I love my family ever so dearly,
And they will always mean the world to me.

School
by David Nguyen

Yesterday I went to school
My mom took me here
Today my mom is at work
My dad took me to class
The smell is great at school
The trees are beautiful
The trees are like an umbrella
like an umbrella to walk to school
My teacher is the best
She is my favorite teacher
She cares about my education
also teaches me about God every day
Oh how I love her forever
Because she is the best
She is to demand to make me great
And saying goodbye to that is hard
I am always trying my best in school
I promise to be successful in 6th grade
I am trying to get good grades
to not let my teachers down.

The Golden Season
by Ivanna Rhodes

When the leaves begin to change,
You know the summer's over.
When the wind's as sharp as a pang
The golden season's just around the corner.
Apples begin to fall,
With their rich cider scent,
They are prepared for feasts,
That are quite pleasant.
The golden-yellow pumpkins,
Sit like small suns in the fields,
The shimmering yellow wheat,
Their fine kernels they yield.
The squashes and potatoes,
Are gathered before frost.
The hard-working farmer,
Works that one crop may not be lost.
The golden season's fruitfulness,
Is prosperous indeed,
And God created it for us,
To meet our every need.

Crickets
by Emma M. Price

As I peer into the dark
And past the campfire's light
I see climbing vines
Tall fruit trees
Broken boards
Wind weathered pots
Swaying daffodils
Growing out of ash
I wonder if the trees were harvested each fall
And if the flowers were cut on an early spring morning
Year and years ago
And if the pots were once shiny and new
But now, broken pieces of lives long gone
Left for fear of the mines buried in the fields
Lie with crumbling walls and burnt husks
The only reminders of a war long forgotten
And I imagine what it was like
So many years ago
But I hear only the crickets

Words
by Shayla Quinlan

What happened to this world?
People so focused on the wrong things.
People talk trash about other people, but never realize words hurt.
That "sticks and stones may break my bones, but words will never hurt me" is a lie.
Words hurt.
People hurt each other every day.
People hurt each other so much that they hurt themselves.
Everybody deserves chances. Everybody deserves life.
Stop just worrying about you.
Worry about people that have no home.
That have no family. That have no food.
Because people are so selfish and focused on themselves.
That they don't realize how special a human life is.
They don't realize it could be worse. You could have no family.
Think about that.
When you tell somebody you hate them and hope they die.
What happens when they're actually gone.
What would you do if the last thing you said to your mother or father.
Sister or brother that you hate them, and just like that they're gone.
Words hurt.

Christmas
by Allie Battle

The snow is falling,
Christmastime is here right now.
My favorite day.

Falling Leaves
by Jacob Wellham

Oh I can't believe the many sights I see,
As warm air turns to a cool breeze.
Shorter days have now begun, summer's on the run,
And we see changing light from the fading sun.
An abundance of trees, once with green leaves,
Become an array of colors that inspiringly please.
As the temperature drops, the color change stops,
We begin harvesting the last of the crops.
What once arose like an ocean of rainbows,
Quickly fades as time goes.
All the colors now the same, appear to have a stain,
Once so beautiful, but now so plain.
Now the trend shows increasing wind,
While we feel winter slowly creeping in.
Falling leaves so brown, scatter to the ground,
Till only empty trees can be found.

Jumbles of Words
by Baylee Peperak

Jumbles of words fill my head like clouds over an Arizona sunset
Silently intertwining themselves into elaborate ideas
And silently pushing my mind to new places.
Jumbles of words flowing like Niagara Falls, slowly
But then falling quickly into place
letting my mind wander into whimsical oblivion.
Jumbles of words like building blocks
attempting to create the 8th Wonder of the World
Thousands of bricks slowly gaining into an intricate dome of ideas
Jumbles of words like a small child in a candy store
overwhelming, but spectacularly wonderful
Beaming with joy and bubbling with excitement.
Jumbles of words like Lake McDonald
Colorful, and vibrant, yet scattered and shattered
Creating an aesthetically pleasing mosaic of wonder.
Jumbles of words that are so different
Yet so alike.

Regret, Fear, and Triumphant of Talking
by Jaden Adwater

I regret talking when
Expectations silent but I
Can't help it I fear that I
Will get in trouble and my
Mouth would run away from
Me because I can't shut up
But one day I would have
a triumphant for closing my mouth

The Sugar Gliders' Amazon Adventure
by Kendell Edwards

His pet sugar gliders live in a cage.
Their owner, Kendell, is eleven years of age.
They all took a long summer journey to the Amazon;
Where in the rain forest, they saw the biggest python.
Kendell got scared and left his gliders behind.
Crawling from their bag, they started to whine.
First, they met a Jesus lizard,
Who walked on water leaving them bewildered.
Next, they met a macaw who could really talk;
He told them where to go and walk.
So, for two hours or more they travelled around;
Until, they caught a plane lifting up from the ground.

Flavors of Fall
by Lindsey Sanders

Looking out of my window I see the colorful trees,
Fall is here, the time of year for flavorful smells and a cool breeze.
No more summer nights, we finally have cool air.
Football games on Friday nights, the cheerleaders are there.
Cinnamon and apples, a trendy fall treat.
Cozying up by the fireplace with fuzzy socks to warm my feet.
Fall is known as the season of "pink,"
As we recognize and continue the fight against a disease that really stinks.
Halloween is near, won't you give a creepy little sneer?
Ghosts, bats, candy and black cats,
Costume parties, tricks and treats, and kids acting like brats.
Finally it's Thanksgiving, the time where family gathers and nothing else matters.
Fathers and mothers make their turkey in the oven,
While the kids play outside with all of their cousins.
The flavors of fall are so vibrant and strong,
I wish the autumn season could last all year long.

Water Bottle
by Andrew Warner

My water bottle is round
It always falls on the ground
My water bottle is green
It's also pretty clean
It's always falling over
I got it from Dover
It always can be found
Because it makes a very loud sound
I like it very much
And it's very cold to the touch

My Love For Jesus
by Sean P. Henderson

Jesus is the center of my life,
His precious words cut sin like a knife.
Every day He provides a lamp to my feet,
So that I can share His love with people I meet.
In His word, He promises never to leave or forsake me,
And in my times of trouble, He is my key.
Whenever I feel alone or afraid,
In my heart, His promises have stayed.
He keeps watch over me every single night,
And as long as I trust in Him, my future will be bright.
That is all for today, tomorrow is new,
In the word of the Lord, there is peace for you.

Ball On My Wall
by Cleveland McAfee

Look at my ball
That's on my wall
It doesn't look fun
Up there all day long
It just sits by itself
I know it's sad every day
By itself on that wall
I feel sad that it's on the wall
That ball might be mad
Because I don't play with it
But now the ball
Is not on the wall
Now it's in my hand
Instead of on the wall.

Cheerleading - Baseball
by Laci Davis

Cheerleading
Fun, tiring
Moving, chanting, encouraging
Jump high, chant loud, player
Sliding, hitting, running
Fast, entertaining
Baseball

My Peaceful Spot
by Clara Atsinger

Of all the places in the wood my favorite is my peaceful spot,
Where storms and trials are overcome in my imagination.
The battle's raged for quite some years,
The heroine takes her bow, arrows fly, hers finds the mark,
My peaceful spot is won.
"Retreat! Retreat! We're all but lost, her peace won't let us in."
Cleared from vice and cleared from fury, now friends of mine can come.
Fairies take up residence, gnomes' hats stand guard around the ring,
Elves arrive to keep it lively, songs and dance their chief delight.
So when I'm sad and tears keep coming, the dappled woods call out my name.
Through gate op' wide, I hurry there to find my stump, my forest shade;
My peaceful spot …

New World
by Ugochukwu Agubokwu

You wake up only to find yourself in an unfamiliar place
You walk around to only figure that you don't know anything about it
Why can't you see a familiar face?
You can't help but explore that "New World"
Feel like having fun, leaving your trace
Marking your territory on everywhere, twirling and being twirled
You then remember that you're trying to remember your purpose
Ask yourself questions, that doesn't even work or make any sense
Have you been reincarnated? Maybe you've been reborn? Have you died?
Maybe you had amnesia, or just can't remember why you're here
We can't all remember that many things that well
But we all can't be perfect
Some of us remember things better than others
But getting back to priority
You just realize your purpose
It's to be happy and live your life in this "New World" and be satisfied with it

Happy Anywhere
by Eliana Amoh

When I walk outside,
I am happy.
Why ...
It makes me feel like I'm part of the world.
Indoors, I am also happy.
Why ...
It makes me feel like I'm in the world.
Anywhere I go, I try to be happy.
Why ...
'Cause this is the world.

Elliot
by Abigail Boyd

Elliot is a very lazy cat,
So he is very fat.
He likes to spend all day,
Finding new spots to lay.
My cat likes to eat,
Especially when you offer him a treat.
Elliot is a scaredy cat,
He's even afraid of a bump in the mat.
He purrs quite loud,
Which makes him feel like a vibrating cloud.
Elliot is a very lazy cat,
And now you know why he is so fat.

The Dark Room
by Rachel Pham

I'm trapped
The gray walls are closing in
I'm panting, I'm scared
Each wall, pushing me from side to side
I'm afraid of moving
Like I haven't moved before
Claws reach out of the walls
Trying to grab me
Dark is all I see
A dark room of emptiness
I can't think properly
I can't calm down
Finally, I wake up from that nightmare
In my bed again

Change
by Brooklyn Potter

As tomorrow comes, the sun goes down
All around you see the town
The flowers bloom, the trees grow green
The fires of winter grow to a dim sheen
The rain drips down
The world wears a golden crown
As time goes by, the people change
There is no more light, only pain
But the world can go back, back to happier times
We just need to stop being mimes
So we can speak the change we want to see in our lifetimes.

My Life
by Keltyn McKinley

My life is a maze
Twisting and turning with haste
But I like to keep it simple and at my own pace
I was born in November
And celebrate that day
I love playing games but in my own way
I don't understand why God loves me so much
But I'm waiting for Him to take me up
I love my friends and play with them every day
But I hate homework just like my duck
I love my duck and feed him a lot
But keep him healthy because I walk him a lot

Home
by Mary Sass

Most say home is where you grew up; they're wrong
Some kids grow up in orphanages and homeless shelters
and say that they would never call it home.
Home can be anywhere
It is the one place where you can express your feelings and not be judged
Some people don't know how to do that;
they end up never letting their emotions out and soon it causes anger and confusion
Explore.
Find a place to call home, express your feelings, thoughts, emotions
let the world know who you are.
If you don't try, you will never know what you can do
Find home.

My Dog
by Abigail Donaldson

My dog likes to lie upside down
She never has a frown
She likes to play with my bunny
She likes to run 'round and 'round
My dog is really funny

Mickey Mouse Cheese
by Ashleigh Peters

This cheese is very cheesy.
It's soft and very cold.
Crackers make it taste the best
And sometimes it will mold.
Cheddar and Mozzarella,
Colby or Monterey Jack.
No matter where you are
It's the perfect snack.
It can go on a sandwich,
Or pizza if you prefer
Nachos, tacos, or burritos too
To make your tummy purr

Guns
by Sa'Real McRae

It's funny that words are like bullets
And our mouths are like guns
that spout out the pellets
at the twist of our tongue.
It's funny that words are like bullets
That our brain is arranged to obtain the things we could say
Load the gun and aim, bang, fire
Hoping the words can explain our true desire.
It's funny that words are like bullets
That one wrong move could end someone's life
One wrong move could be a genocide
That words can be shot at you so quickly
You barely have time to react
Before you know it you're on the ground
Dying, as a matter of fact.
It's funny that words are like bullets.
The words are our bullets
Our mouth is our gun
We've all got a loaded gun at the tips of our tongues

Gold
by Isabelle Christine Hoge

Nobody is ordinary, everybody's extraordinary
We all dream way past the stars, even farther than Mars
Nobody is less than another, we all are equal to each other
We all form the world
Everybody would come together, share happiness and peace forever
But sometimes you feel like bronze not gold
But you shouldn't think that because you know you are gold

My Sister and I
by Ana Morlier

My sister and I, my greatest friend,
She will always be mine, until the end.
We've triumphed and failed,
She was always there, so I prevailed.
I've stepped on her toes, she's stepped on mine,
We've argued and fought, some of the time.
We laugh and play, fight and sulk,
I'll make her pay for her insults.
She's supportive of me, through thick and thin,
And she'll always be with me, until the end.

My Wonderful Pajamas
by Isabella Collier

I love my pajamas
They are silly
They are comfortable
They are soft
They are colorful
They are messy
They make me sleepy
They keep me warm from head to toe.
I can play in the dirt with them
I can eat breakfast in them
I can even eat dinner in them
I can run in them
I can read in them
I can even watch TV in them
I just wish I could wear them forever.

Universal
by Geoffrey Taylor

Universe of fun
Nothing is horrible, not even the 4D theaters
Infinite joy everywhere at the Islands of Adventure
Very awesome at the Wizarding World of Harry Potter
Experience magic everywhere you go
Really funny experience of Duff in the
Simpsons' area
Adventure is around every corner
Let's go to Universal some time.

Weather
by Sarah Shivers

I look out my window, rain is pouring down.
Everyone's asleep, not even a sound
A look at news, the weatherman said,
"A thunderstorm is coming, get out of the bed."
Mom and Dad get up and get me and my siblings
We head down to the basement, as the thunder is rumbling
Safe and sound in the basement, we sit calm and quiet.
We have lots of food, but my sister is on a diet.
Listening with our ears, the storm calms down.
Everybody goes up to bed, not even a sound.

Silent Killer
by Terrilyn Lynum-Williams

Yearning of families, such loud sorrow
a melodious sound to my ear
Engulfed by disease today and tomorrow
As they try to escape the death that lurks here
Loved ones fade until they are no more
Little ones scream in a loud screeching horror.
Off to somewhere else says their chief
We will rebuild another far from here
While my victims stay in pain and grief
I will triumph and dance and cheer
Fool! You cannot escape my grasp
Even though of your family you are the last
Look at victims spread across the streets
Lying dead as silence sweeps
My victims' souls spread the good news for me
For here I am, the silent killer of 1793

Hurricane Matthew
by Autumn Gault

In the storm, it was all kinds of warm
On that stormy night, it was such a fright
The wind howled, the trees growled
I didn't know what was happening, all the trees keep snapping
The light snapped off and the news went off
I was so scared, I could not bear
The sound of thunder in the air
Then it all stopped, no more power lines popped
Then we went outside, we were so surprised
All the damage and despair, and all lives taken everywhere

School Spirit
by Madeline Mayo

What's really the point of school? To learn, to talk, to play all day,
what do we do at school anyway?
Put down the phones, pick up the pencils, that's the spirit! Now you've got it!
Kids are stuck in failing schools, with no discipline or rules.
But who cares? Not them. Do you?
Our generation will ruin this nation. Will we make it?
Don't blame us, you're the ones that raised us!
So leave us here, erase your past,
for this generation will not last without school spirit!

EXTRAordinary
by Emma Schurr

I'm a grain of sand in the beach of the world.
Not special, just one of many.
I do my best to stand out like others.
Waiting and watching to prove myself different.
But every time I try, so does everyone else.
So I go out of my way to be the strongest, fastest, and smartest
to show I'm unique. But I can't. I'm too scared.
What if I work so hard to achieve nothing?
Do I have power to fight being ordinary?
To fight the world?
I don't care that I'm scared.
I saddle up on the horse of adventure.
To figure out what makes me, me.
To find out what I'm living for.
I plan to never stop.
I'm too terrified to try but I do it anyway.
That is what makes me brave.
That is what makes me, me.

Me
by Donnetra Freeman

Who am I, A dreamer, A hard worker, 12 year old, Me
The youngest, A thinker, 6th grader, Me,
A sister of a 24 year old, An A and B student, A foodie, Me,
I am a beautiful girl with big dreams, With a big heart, God lover, Me,
Two loving parents, Graphic designer and who break their back for me,
Me

Spring's Almost Over
by Zylaysha Myers

Spring's almost over, school letting out
Kids going crazy and running all about
Spring's almost over, going to the beach
Playing at the park, just hanging around and all about
Spring's almost over, leaves growing back
Flowers blooming everywhere and listening to the ducks quack
Spring's almost over, the weather is hot
Perfect for planting, vacations and cookouts
There are many more but I'll stop right there
Spring's almost over

Coming In Clutch
by Nathan Caldwell

We set up the field
with our coach named Drew
During pre-game warm ups
the other team came all dressed in blue
Both teams chose captains
The referee flipped a coin
We won the toss and wanted the ball
On the kickoff their kicker hurt his groin
The ball went to the end-zone for a touchback
On the first play our receiver caught the ball with ease
During our other plays we got nothing
We decided to punt but the ball got stuck in the trees
When the blue team had the ball
our defense let them score
We got the ball back and took the lead
Our defense didn't let them score anymore
In the fourth quarter we led by two
Now with ten seconds left
the other team needs a field goal
Now with the field smelling like sweat the field goal is blocked, "thump"

Untitled
by Mallory Mathews

Pinkish leaves budding,
Flowers blooming all over
Bearing sweet cherries.

Favorite Animal
by Kylie McGuire

Fox
Sly, cunning
Stalking, lying, waiting
Terrorizing all is prey
Pouncing, chasing, catching
Quiet, red
Animal

The River
by Madeline Parks

The river travels over stones
Rushing thousands of miles
Every day.
The river falls onto stones
Pouring thousands of gallons
Every day
The river carries small stones
Holding thousands of pounds
Every day
The river meets the ocean
Depositing thousands of stones
Every day

The Walk
by Edward Taggart

Once my dog and I were walking to my grandmother's house.
We decided to take the long way.
When we started walking, I smelt something, it smelt horrible.
My dog started barking after he found a dead squirrel.
The squirrel felt wet and it looked like someone shot it.
I pushed it off the road with a stick I found.
Then we continued on and about 20 minutes later we had arrived.
My feet hurt by that time.
Grandma had made some cookies and they were delicious.
I guess it was worth the walk.

Summary
by Caroline Carver

Summer is my favorite season
I can give you all the reasons
It is so much fun
Playing in the sun
I hope you don't think I'm teasin'

Queen of Hearts
by Sarah King

There once was a Queen of Hearts
She did nothing but tear you apart
She gave you one look
And your life she took
That crazy old Queen of Hearts

Peace
by Juliana Nguyen

Peace is the key to life
You could have a wife or a knife to keep you peaceful in life
Roses are red, violets are blue
stay peaceful like a moon in the sky
You could cry or deny or be high
but always be in the sky where the sunrise starts
You could have a part of a heart but still remember to have peace in your life
You could take pills or pay bills but never forget to be clever forever
Never forget that peace is the key to life

Tinker
by Shreya Sudakar

The workshop is cluttered with assorted parts of curious devices
His slender fingers work nimbly assembling metal pieces
Flames lick at the steel, binding it together
The mechanic sits at the desk, his back hunched over his contraption
A click resounds, the man straightens
He admires the creation he has made, looking at it with satisfaction
As he turns the winder no chiming music is to be heard
He slams his fist down in frustration, all his hard work gone to waste
But he lets out a sigh and goes back to tinkering

All In My Head
by Oluwadasola Abatan

Under my bed there is something dead
Scary sounds that I think are all in my head
A white ghost
Being tonight's host
Blood on a knife
That once killed a wife
A demon walking around
Standing tall on the ground
Killing anyone that comes into his bound
I walk into a haunted house
As I walk I see a bloodstained blouse
With an evil bloodstained razor sharp teeth mouse
I feel like death was coming to my future spouse
I feel something breathe against my cheeks
I stand to my feet
Ready to meet
What I needed to defeat

Sage and the Girl
by Salim Babaji

He used to meet her every day
He loved her to the end of his days
This girl was a dream come true
She was the only one who didn't think Sage was a fool
The boy named Sage she called and shout
When they were together there was no doubt
They loved each other with all their hearts
And they say loved can always be achieved
But for this was a lie
Sage had been deceived
The girl he loved and saw and trusted
Was just a dream
Sage woke up on his pitiful bed
Looked up to his ceiling and sadly said
Love is a lie, deceit and cheat, just look how love just treated me
For Sage was lonely
He remembered his dream
He remembered the sweet girl Natalie
For then he promised with all his heart
He would never forget what tore apart

The Moon
by Asma Mohammed

It glows,
Subtly,
Enhancing the gloomy night.
It's a nightlight
In a child's bedroom.
A helper;
Guiding the people of the night.
Beautiful.
Its lavishing glimmers
Of tender white and buttery yellow.
It suspends in the starry, night sky,
Watching.

Indescribable
by Alanna Avery

Indescribable, sweet and true
Oh wonderful Papa, I love you
Every task that must be done
Papa made it so much fun
Oh the joyful words he gave
All the memories I must save
Spiritual advice when it's needed
Cheered for me when I succeeded
Picked me up when I felt blue
Indescribable Papa, I love you

A Dream
by Teryn Winn

A dream is something you hold on to
No matter what you go through.
A dream is something that you strive to achieve
And what you have always believed in.
A dream is something that can be big or small
But to you it is worth it all.
A dream is something you will never abandon
For your dream you will stand.
A dream is real and true
And it means so much to you.
So ... dream your dream
And do not be afraid
Because you can do anything.

Maryland
by Wyatt Dooley

My favorite state
Awesome stuff to do
Red, black, and yellow flag
Your U.S.A capital, Washington, DC
Learn something new every day
Annapolis is Maryland's capital
New stuff to do
Decorated flag

Society
by Elise Flurry

Society, basically telling us who we're supposed to be
we're all different you see
we all laugh, love, live, learn,
discourage the ones we love most, only losing hope
words stick like glue, sometimes they are true
but can cause a world of pain
feeling ashamed when we should not
causing depression and deadly thoughts
wishing we could be someone else
thinking we are different in a bad way
no one to tell us, "It's going to be ok"
Who are you to think you can tell us who to be?
I guess that's just society

Archery
by Sean Lee

The crisp, clean targets lined up in perfect order
and a silver bow shimmering in the morning air ready to be shot
I can smell the cool, dewy air
and the scent of pristine equipment, empty of imperfection
I can feel the tense, nervous grip on my bow,
and sense the pressure as I draw back for the thousandth time
Time seems to stop as I carefully peer through my sight,
practicing the form I have memorized soundly
The sharp, sudden snap of the bow and an arrow whistling through the air,
swiftly finding its mark in a sea of yellow
I can feel my heart beating wildly in my chest and my breath catching in my throat
as I wait in anticipation, ready for any outcome
The satisfaction and relief of victory as I accept my gold medal
and see the smiles of my teammates and coach
Archery is truly a sport worth playing

All Dear Lives
by Norah Wilson

War
Everything is war
The anti-Semitism has reached its boiling point
I'm not a Jew
But I feel part of them more than ever
Because my loved ones or greatest friends
could be Jew
Not telling anyone
Living in the ghetto
Going to concentration camps
Crying
Nobody listening
Nobody caring
No one but Yahweh (God)
This is the Holocaust.

Sisters
by Reine Brezial

Watch them play around together
They remind me of a bird chasing its feather
I watch them play dress-up
When one is sad, the other says, "Don't let them see you cry, girl pick yo head up"
They will tell each other about boyfriends
They will have secret parties and would regret saying, "Come in!"
(They would take the blame for each other)
They will throw grapes in each other's mouth
But the one thing we all hate about their relationship, is when they fight and shout

Autumn's Swirling Brilliance
by Hannah Vander Wall

Misty gray clouds drift lazily across the gorgeous sky, and along with the breeze,
Which is whistling through the trees, comes the smell of fresh-baked pumpkin pie!
Oh! the colors galore! Blazing yellows-oranges-reds!
Green will not be seen again until next spring, around the bend,
Leaves are swirling 'round your feet and candy corn is awaiting you- a treat!
The wind plays teasingly with the leaves that are scattered all over the ground,
And children frolic in piles of debris that their parents have so patiently raked,
And squirrels frisk 'round in the tall oak trees while scrumptious apple pie is baked!
But amidst all the leaves, laughter, and fun,
All people can look to God, the Holy One,
Whose brilliance has a beauty- the wonderful season of fall.

The Beach
by Bailey O'Barr

I smell the ocean air
The sand is in my hair
I play in the water
As sun is getting hotter
I write words in the sand
And watch them slowly wash away
I look at the water
And watch it day by day
When the wind howls
I slowly close my eyes
And breathe in that salty air
While the waves go by
While the days slowly pass
I think about the sea
What is really out there?
And will I be able to see?
I think really hard,
And hope really good
Please, please
I really think I could

The Star Wars Guy
by Preston Jackson

There once was a guy,
One who knew a lot about the sky
He saw battles
And the sky rattled
There were explosions
And implosions
There was a lot going on
It went on and on
The sky's treasure
Was hard to measure
The guy called it Star Wars
It wasn't a chore
First Order
And the Jedi Order
What was this language
And why
They had a name for him
The Star Wars guy
To be continued …

Hawaii
by Elijah Brewer

Always sunny, Beautiful flowers
Clams on the shore
Diamonds in the sky
Erupting with color
Fire on the beach at night;
Glorious sunset, Happy sunrise
Insects on blades of grass
Jumping over waves near shore;
Kicking dancing everywhere, Loving each other every day;
Morning breeze through my window
Nighttime music loud and clear;
Over waves, Peace and Quiet
Running to the beach with friends;
Surfing waves, Tides come in, Under the starry night;
Very joyful
Winning prizes
Xylophone playing by the fire
Yellow sun
Zzz the sound of sleep.

A Week In Hawaii
by Marcel Williams

Amazing
Beautiful beaches
Crazy night parties
Dancing hula girls
Evolutions
Flowers blooming
Glorious sky
Hawaiian pizza
Igneous rock
Koo koo birds
Luaus
Musical instruments playing
Party every day
Quiet oceans at night
Resting every day
Sounds of birds chirping
Volcanoes spewing magma
Whales in the ocean making amazing sounds

American
by Paul Ward

American pride
Our great country is for all
Homeland country pride

Lights Out!
by Jane Farr

It's time to go to bed at night
And blow out the bright candlelight.
Oh why, oh why, is it me now,
When the clock is chiming so loud?
All are asleep at ten o'clock,
Now I'm the only left awake.
Tomorrow I will be so tired,
I so hope sleep will be acquired.
When finally my sleep will come,
It will be timed on the clock 'one.'
It is now morning-time, and say,
I'm not as tired as I thought I'd be!

What's My Name
by Jayde Hood

Hey there I am Jayde
J-A-Y-D-E
It is an ancient gem
To the Chinese
You may have heard of it
It is a Greenish-blue
The original spelling is J-A-D-E
But that is pretty too
No one really knows about it
It is really rare
It takes many years to form
It's truly a beauty to wear
My Y is important
It's what makes me unique
There is no one else like me
That's why I'm so chic
I am me
That is final
Jayde is Jayde
And I say that with a smile

Julia McNairy

Autumn
by Julia McNairy

Autumn swoops in
in a gorgeous gossamer gown
filled with colors as deep and dark as the sea
as merry and happy as a July sun
she casually waltzes by
knowing the world sighs and wonders at her beauty
Then with a gust of wind and a flourish
she strips the leaves from their branches
to decorate the cold earth
in the colors that reflect
the feeling of summer coming to a close
And as she departs
her work finished
knowing she will have to wait until next year
to be glorified and beloved by all the beauty lovers
in this cold cruel world
she sends the first frost
as her last effort
to let them shiver and quake
to know she will be back next year.

Isabel Yates

Hope
by Isabel Yates

Hope is a wildfire
starting in the barren lands
of melancholy and despair.
Something sparks:
a flicker of faith,
an ember of promise.
It could extinguish, never to return.
Or it could ignite,
casting light
on the darkness
of desperation
and filling the emptiness
of rejection.
The once small spark,
now a wildfire,
spreading through the vast regions
of our minds
and enveloping all traces of loss,
till all that is left is hope:
a wildfire of hope

1st Place

Alexander Ashman

Alexander submitted his poem, "The Sea"
while in the 7th grade.
He enjoys reading,
along with creative writing,
and certainly possesses a flair for the descriptive.
Nice job, Alexander!

The Sea
by Alexander Ashman

The sea is that of a thousand swans
Drinking upon the billows
From her lips, she brews a frothy bliss
Rest your head into her pillow
Her hair ripples in the breeze
Her eyes are knowing and plain
She's experienced joy and laughter
But suffering just the same
You can hear her emerald giggle
In the caw of midnight gulls
Her lullabies soothe the sky
To sleep, as well as wooden hulls
You can tell her all your secrets,
Whisper them in her ear
She grins and flips her moistened hair
As daylight disappears
"Good night!" she cries to the setting sun
She puts the world at ease
"To bed," she says with a flashing wink
"There's another day to seize."

Division III

Grades
8-9

Pompeii
by Rachel Eaton

The land was pure, cleansed.
Cleansed as white as a bride waiting for her groom.
Pure and unstained by the travesties of man.
The land built by man is stained once more, but not by man alone.
Ashes, ashes fell down from the boundless sky,
coming upon the land, like an unforeseen kiss.
The ash rained down dancing about chaotically,
at the fearful wonder planted in the watching eyes below.
Fearful wonder was soon forgotten as the eyes turned not to the sky,
but to the land they were bound to by race and blood.
To the land mass ahead, spewing its crimson fury.
Final breaths are taken, a final heartbeat teasing mortality.
City on fire, city on fire the land fell to flame.
Hell had come on Earth to play, but not a game of chance.
The bountiful work of man was undone, and the land was cleansed once more,
cleansed by the ashes of man.
From the ashes they rose, as ashes they fell.
The dust settles over the rubble, the final ashes of man
blowing over the winding hills.
God had held no mercy for man, woman, nor child,
for the walls had tumbled down, the city had fallen.
Man became relics of old, in that town, Pompeii.

A Fragile Thing Called Life
by Jasmine Swaby

A breath of life can be given or taken
No matter how hard we try it's not our decision
It can bring tears of happiness
And definitely ones of sadness
We can cradle it a lot, but bad things will happen
We grip it with the fear that death will soon be near
Because most of us envision it with a cold stare and a sneer
But sometimes we don't care about it as much as we should
We throw it into fires as if it was wood
Words
It can make a person give away the precious gift that they were given
All because of one other's decision
We walk on glass
Once we see a friend's life slowly slipping through their grasp
But if they were to be in a different class
Would we care, would we ask?
A breath of life, it can be taken or given
And once it's gone
Will we regret our decision?

Demons and Angels
by Katelyn Scherrer

Worry is like a demon,
Running wild in your mind
You never wonder what's ahead, only what's behind.
Your angels are like shadows, in a dim-lit light
Only faintly there like silhouettes in the night.
You're in a world of darkness, where you can't find the light
You try to climb your way up, but your demons put up a fight
You always try to beat them, but your angels run and hide.
It's like a broken record, playing again and again
You want the record to break, but it's your only friend.
You put another fake smile on your face, to hide all of your fears
You lie and say that it's alright, but they can't see the tears
You finally let the river flow after all of these years.
You can't make one mistake or your walls will come crumbling down
You're so scared to let go and fall and hit the ground.
But don't worry because one day your hard work will pay off
Your demons will be gone and your angels will be strong,
You will finally break the chains that hold you down,
But don't worry, you will fly,
You will not fall and hit the ground.

Pieces of Me
by Hadiyah Graham

You may see me as one whole thing
However, I am many of a name
My brain, my heart, my bones, my guts
Are pieces of me
My soul, my energy, my aura
Are pieces of me
My mind, my emotions, my thinking
Are pieces of me
My personality, my charm, my nature
Are pieces of me
My strength, my weaknesses, my corrections, my mistakes
Are pieces of me
My name, my birthday, my age
Are pieces of me
My family, my friends, my home
Are pieces of me
My people, my country, my world
Are pieces of me
Now that you see as many of a name
You may see me as one whole thing

The Cat
by Resa Robinett

There once was a cat, and his name was Pat
He wore a fabulous hat, but when he saw a bat he began to scat
When Pat got home, he began to roam
When his hair got stuck in a comb, he began to moan
He slept in a dome, so when he left his home, he ate a bone
He went to the store and he bought a boar
After he went to Doctor Moore, that made him poor
Then he felt rotten to the core.

If You
by Kaitlin T. Drake

If dreaming of you is warmth, I'll be cold
If loving you heals me, I'll die
If seeing you heals me, I'll stay wounded
If hearing your name completes me, I'd rather be incomplete
If thinking of you calms me, I'd rather be stressed out
If talking to you will make me happy, I'll be depressed
If knowing you strengthens me, I'll be weak
If remembering you is a hello, I'll want to say goodbye
If being with you is my safety, I want to be in danger
If you were anything to me, I was nothing at all to you

Let's Be Free
by Autumn DuPre

Who wants to be free up in a tree, thinking oh what's not to like of being free
where no one tells you what to be, what to do and how to be and how you do.
We grow up so fast, it won't last because most of the time we're in school
so I think of the beautiful world, you just want to look up in the sky
and then fly and be free just like the blue sea,
fish swimming around the water freely in the clear water.
Adventurous is so generous, wandering around being yourself
curiosity and that place where no one can tell you what to do and how to do it.
Just wandering in that free mind of yours.
Where you're not controlled just being you.
When it's fall I like the cool breeze blowing on me and my hair
then the tall shadow behind me. You also see birds soaring through the air
and you care because you want to be like that one day,
flying fast with that nice cool wind blowing in your face
then when the sunset goes down you fly to the nearest big sigh and sit there
and watch the beautiful orange pink puffy looking clouds, sunset going down
until night comes when it's cold and all the birds go back to their nest like we do
and go to sleep in the cool warm nest.

Rocks
by Dhabriah Askew

Rocks, rocks, one after one you throw at me.
Pain unbearable, excruciating pain you cause on me.
But for you I reach out my hand to grab you, to lift you up,
even though you've hurt me many times before I still am here for you.
Rocks, more rocks, pain more pain,
but as you grow you shall see how much pain you cause me.
Pain will be no more, just you and me.

Gone
by Sage Wann

With a bird's eye view of the world
And words whistle through trees like wind
Darkness slowly creeps in between shadows
And discouragement will swallow you whole
The sound of laughter, and a cry for help
Quietly echoes down the halls
Searching through a hundred doors
Down a hundred halls
Only to find that you're still lost
Lost and gone with the wind
But being gone welcomes you
Being gone is a beautiful thing

Beautiful Blindness
by Josie Bain

The world is a wonderful place.
Many people don't just stop and look around while walking home anymore.
The world was once a beautiful place until technology came and destroyed it.
iPhones are like a disease, once it starts it can't be stopped.
Many people are blind to what is right in front of them unless it's their phone.
The most amazing things on Earth could be a blade of grass or a ray of sunshine.
The world is a wonderful place.
The world is a wonderful place.
Your phone screen is not real, it is a jumble of pixels.
A field of flowers is not made of pixels it is real, it is forever.
A thumb pushing down can make everything change,
but only disasters can change the Earth.
The Earth is fresh and clean.
A phone is used over and over, covered in hand grease.
The world is forever my home.
I can't live without the Earth but I could live without a phone.
The world is a wonderful place.

The Mustang Is Born
by Brandon Winn

There once was a horse
Who was born unnamed
He was not bred the same as any other game
As the horse grew older
It was stronger than others, and much bolder.
It was desperate and relentless
It was wild and tameless
It was a brave, tough and a strong animal
It was named ... the mustang.

A Friend's Love
by Tia Winn

There is great joy in having a friend
Someone who you love and trust in
A friendship is an honor
and a promise you must keep
A friend helps you stay in place
And keeps you on your feet
Friends give a friendly love
to help you make it through
Sometimes no one but a mother could ever do
Friends create a bond to stick to and hold
This bond will keep them until they're very old

There's Always a Hope
by Isaac Melo

When you're at your darkest times
and you feel you're breaking down,
when the sparkle drains from your eyes
and you feel you're going to drown,
there's hope, there's always hope.
Express it, feel it, don't hold it down.
let it thrive, it will make you feel alive,
put a smile on your face, take away that frown.
That moment you will realize,
there is hope, there will always be hope.
After a while of being in the ditch,
the ditch of sadness and fear,
this hope will make you feel rich,
it will make your conscience clear.
And in your final moments you will realize,
there's always a hope.

True Vision/True Acuity
by Jackson Futrell

There is a sure and constant motion, only seen, only felt, on the ocean
I see such vastness, it is black, it is the bluest turquoise, the greenest emerald green
I see what is happening, what is building to happen, as they crash and pull back,
the waves of the sea
I see the tiny life forms, tasty morsels, as they beach touching the sand
And the larger ones never touching land
I see as only a seagull can
Whether standing on the shoreline or on the bow
I can see, looking with true vision/true acuity
I not only see the seagull but I have the ability to see as he sees
What a great world it would be if all humanity could truly see
Not only as self sees but also as others see- true vision/true acuity

Into a Daydream
by Emma Holston

In my dreams of night, I may have no control on what I see.
In my dreams of day, however, I have full rule ...
I am queen of all I possibly imagine.
My conscience is my fortress, my mind's eye the inhabitant.
In a dark lonely place, my thoughts begin to multiply,
rapidly soaring as new dreams begin.
And though I know I shouldn't ignore the tedious repetition
of the day's lectures and withholds,
I can't help but indulge in the escape that is the possibility of joy freedom poses.
My thoughts, a flock of individual, uniquely painted birds,
soar wildly over fields of memories, gliding into the abyss of imagination;
that land of former memories and endless possibilities.
Welcomed fiends weasel their way to my conscience
to free me from my imprisoned reality,
Reaching out to me just in time from slipping, falling down
into the painful depths of boredom; it's insanity in my case.
Dreams come at horrible, yet impeccable times,
while my peers around me pay attention; not me, though.
My mind is in a place over thousands of miles, years, possibilities away:
I'm crashing over rough, black waters, grasping my sword on the deck of my ship,
I'm searching my way blindly through a dense forest,
sweet scents of clear air breezing by, I'm bareback on a stunning steed,
splashing joyously through the currents of a shallow river.
Though awakening from these dreams,
I'm caught where I was before; lost in the dreaded real.
And away from freedom I'm ripped forcefully
until I may meet back with my imagination,
That which keeps me from giving in to insanity;
delivered to a place I can truly be myself ... into a daydream.

Be Kind!
by Marquis Burton

It's so cool to be kind!
It starts right here with me ...
Just cool to be kind,
Sprinkle kindness and see!
It's cool to be kind,
NOT kind, to be rude ...
'cause I will pay you no mind,
and say "go away," I don't have time ...

The Outdoors
by Donathan Fabie

A place to think about all of your sins
A place to think about your rights or wrongs
A place to clear your mind
The place I know like the back of my hand
As I sit there, baking in the autumn sun
I slowly drift off in my thoughts
Listening to the autumn breeze
Shuffling through the mid-autumn trees
I now cringe at the thought of my wrongs
And now realize what had gone wrong
I now realize that's all in the past
Now I can focus on what could happen next
After all my thinking, I have now realized
I can right all of my wrongs and start over

Hola
by Claire Bowman

Ella me dice "Hola."
Una palabra que puede empezar una relación.
Una palabra que puede romper una relación.
Una palabra que puede en contrar a un amigo para tí,
pero que también puede encontrar un enemigo.
A la traición le gusta esconderse en las personas que tú amas.
Se convierte la luz en la oscuridad.
Se convierte el valor en miedo.
Vuelve la espalda de tus amigos y da sus sonrisas a alguien más.
Pero traición también te enseña.
Te enseña quienes son tus amigos.
Te enseña quienes son tus enemigos.
Te enseña cómo ser una mejor persona y ayudar a las personas como tú.
Miras una niña pequeña, sola, y asustada, y a ella le dices "Hola."

El Mar Majestuoso
by Arham Alam

El mar es muy majestuoso.
Tiene muchos peces.
Iba al mar muchas veces.
Pero ahora quieroir
Otra vez.
El mar es más tranquilo que la ciudad.
Y es un paraiso.

Winter
by Vianne Galban

I listen to the wind howl outside my window
As I awake, I sit up in my bed
I peek out the window to see a blanket of clean white snow
The snow is still falling
The small flakes of ice land peacefully on the ground
I watch for a while when I see a black cat walk across the lawn
Little footprints are left in its wake
I quickly get up wrapping my blanket around me
The door creaks open and I step out onto the porch
The cat looks up at me amd gives a faint "meow"
I walk closer and caress it in my blanket
I walk back inside with the cat in my arms
The winter snow brings a new day and a new member in my family

Seasons
by Gwendolyn Zorc

Blazing warmth, heated sand
Sunrise wakes the sleeping land
Children splash in the rising sun
Never quitting 'til the day is done
Lively pigments, gentle breeze
Light shines through the vibrant leaves
Pumpkins carved, lovers gaze
Strolling through the dark corn maze
Gingerbread houses, ice skates laced
Heat rises from the fireplace
Naked branches, chilling air
Wardrobes burst with layered wear
Sunshine smiles, bunnies frolic
Children play while flowers are picked
Dandelions blossom, blue birds fly
Soaring through the sunset sky

Krispy Kreme
by Stephen Bowden

The only treat I want to eat,
Is as soft as a pillow and sugary sweet.
Glazed or powdered, either way,
I could sit home and eat them all day.
A white and green box makes me so glad.
I have to hide them from my mom and dad.
To have a store would be a dream.
I want to own a Krispy Kreme.

Letters of 1943
by Molly Poland

One letter can represent so much,
if only he was here to touch.
While I read his wonderful letter,
thinking of his spirit made me feel better.
Way back when he was here,
he wrote them to me, his dear.
1942, when the war was at its worst,
2,448 soldiers were stationed first.
That day, December of 1943,
I went to my mailbox to see a special letter waiting on me.
John, his best friend, whom the letter was from,
I wasn't expecting what was to come.
"I am so sorry for your loss," I couldn't believe,
oh, how much grief in that letter of 1943.

Oh What a Wonderful Day It Is
by Thorne Crews

It was a horrible day.
There was yelling, screaming,
and nothing but a bunch of fuss while riding on the school bus.
There was a little laughing, clapping and people in the back rapping,
others were just pencil tapping.
Then there was hitting and slapping which made some people mad and others sad.
Kids were getting moved to the front because they were being bad.
Some of the kids were good, doing what they should,
trying to do as much good as they could.
Then the sun came out and the sky turned blue and I started feeling good too.
Because I just got my report card and I got three A's and three B's.
I didn't get a single C or D
and I didn't know how good this day would eventually be.
But all I can say is, "Oh what a wonderful day it is."

Everyone Is Perfect
by Sara Jaramillo

Everyone is different.
Everyone has a thing that makes them special.
Why change that?
Everyone has a family that loves them for who they are.
Everyone has a secret talent.
Why hide that?
Everyone has a personality that makes people happy.
Everyone is perfect being themselves.
Don't change that.

Namaste
by Brooke Maulden

I met a sweet lady walking down the street
Her greeting was short, it was also very sweet
I will never forget the wrinkles in her face
Or the way she talked with the calmness of her voice
I never thought to acknowledge what she said to me
Until one thing she spoke will always stick with me
She explained of great beauty, of things ever so pure
Until the things made sense more and more
She told me to be careful of people in the world
Before she left she held my hand and said
Namaste, Namaste, beautiful young girl.

Color Block
by Judy Zhou

She sits before the mirror and stares
at the reason of her rejection.
A face cloaked in smooth,
chocolatey darkness stares back.
And when she digs her nails
deep into her flawed skin with frustration-
she slowly, but surely
begins tearing it off her frame little by little.
And when all that's left
is the brightness of bone
and the rosiness of muscle-
She rolls on a disguise of white.
And when she returns the next day
skin painted with ivory,
her ears ring with the word she so badly craved-
"yes."

War
by Fernando Avila

An act with no embodiment
Only triggering suffering and hostility
Thousands are put to death
Which has congested our graveyards with silent breaths
Many more are haunted with terrible memories
Why can't we breathe in peace?
In a world of unity that causes violence to cease
So that the battlefield is not a river of blood and sacrifice
But a field abundant with health and happiness of our own device

We Know All Too Well
by Kamryn Bowling

You say you're okay. You say that you're fine.
You say it's nothing; not to worry at all.
We know all too well that this is not you.
You used to speak. You used to smile.
You seem so cold now. We know something's wrong.
We know you're not fine. You rarely speak.
We want to know why. You say you trust us.
You say you have told us everything, but we know that's not true.
After all, we are your friends. We know all too well.
I promise, we shall not tell. Now, please, tell us what has changed.

One's Knowledge of Poetry
by Nihya Dejene

A rhyme on words or no rhymes due
Words that mean powerful meanings, meanings that feel or are true
Poetry to me is like music or a guide in our lives
You take words and make them into something amazing
All of these blazing feelings flowing out of one
The next thing you know, you're staring at a paper filled with meaning and direction
Poems with heart, nice and sweet and deep
How amazing is poetry?
Way beyond what you're thinking, it's beautiful thoughts
Beautiful creativity and more wrapped into one white sheet right in front of you
How enlightening, your writing that I'm spying
It's so alive, it's art
Can't hide what you, your pencil and mind will coincide
All this is, is pride in your line
And sometimes a guide for us that will never hide
So amazing how poetry is to me and how amazing it could be

Mabley, the Balloon
by Charlotte Wilcox

Once there was a balloon
A balloon like no other
It wanted to go to the moon
Unlike another
The balloon's name was Mabley
But no one liked her name
In fact no one liked her lately
The other balloons thought she was lame
But it didn't matter
Because she believed
That she could build a ladder
And then try and leap
Mabley began to build
She worked hard for days
It was as big as a football field
As the stars began to gaze
Her dream was almost true
As she worked through the night
Mabley now saw the moon
Along with the incredible light

Fish Life
by Ridley White

Wonder what fish do?
If only you knew.
In and out their toys,
they swim with grace and poise.
They communicate with bubbles,
and they live with no troubles.
They are always on the look,
for a person or a hook.
Leave if you must,
they'll throw a party at dusk.
They hide behind a log
and stare at the dog.
Wishing they could run
and have that much fun.
At the end of the day,
they are done with play.
They wait to get fed,
but soon, time for bed.
The life of a fish
isn't as you wish.

She/Her
by Flora Smith

She smiles with purpose
Laughs with meaning
She's a bit nervous
But her eyes are gleaming
Her hands fidget
But look at her smile
This is legit
Laughing all the while
She is in love
With the world and her life
She flies like a dove
Her joy is rife
She is everything right
Like a favorite song
She is so bright
I am everything wrong
When it comes to me, she is outdistance
Leaves my mind in a blur
Because she loves existence
And I love her

For My Daddy
by Etoyae Pennington

Sometimes it hurts so much
I can't seem to carry on,
Is he with his siblings?
In that place way up high?
They say he's always watching,
One day he'll come back and say,
"I came back to be with you"
I really miss my daddy,
keeping him from harm
but I'll never forget his smile.
I'll never understand
Why your time was small,
but I hope and pray
I'll see you again some day.
I guess it wasn't meant to be,
your work here was done,
now your life in Heaven
has just begun.
Tears that fall and prayers
will go very far
to reach my loving daddy.

Basketball
by Tatyanna Boatman

In this game your problems are the court.
Your enemies are your opponent.
The ball and team are your everything.
No matter how good or bad you perform.
You always make sure you do your best!
Whatever happens stays on the court.
You are a conqueror!

Like a Dream
by Sravya Chittaluru

One moment it is there,
The next moment, gone.
If I could capture it,
It would be in a book or song.
Hold it close to your heart,
Before it falls apart.
Let it dance all around you,
Let it move and jump like I do.
Have it explore and grow,
But be sure you know,
That this feeling won't stay,
It will be like a dream,
But far, far away.

So Much Life
by Daiyanna Cooper

There is so much life
Why does most of it have to be dark
There are shootings, gangs, and more
Light needs to be shined
When there is darkness there can't be light
People don't know what had become of this world
This needs to be fixed
This is not the world I was born into
There is no sun
It always seems like there is only a moon
The sun needs to be able to shine
There is too much of one thing
People have too much greed in life
Nothing comes out good
This thing can't help anyone
This life needs to be fixed

Disappear
by Jazzmyn Silvers

I close my eyes as I begin to sleep
Looking for a place my dreams will keep
I close my eyes as I sit and weep
Wishing never to wake from this sleep
I walk around in a daze
Underneath their harshest gaze
Nothing ever seems okay
As they watch me wither away
They don't know the pain so deep
They don't see me as I weep
Never again will they say
That I should go away
Leave this Earth and disappear
Watching as I lose all fear

My Dream, My Reality
by Kayleigh Emberton

I started the sport when I was little,
never did I think I would grow to love it the way I do.
Softball, the dirt on my new cleats, the smell of peanuts around the park,
and the cries of fans, cheering on their daughters.
The swing of the bat, the soaring yellow ball, the runners sprinting to the next base,
how does that make me so happy. I get nervous when I go up to bat
but then I hear my team cheering me on, I gain confidence, I am having fun.
Swing and it's gone, I run down the baseline and hear the cheers from the stand.
When I get out on field and tag a runner out on a run down, my team cheers for me.
Those moments make me love softball, those moments make me want to do it
forever. How though, how am I , one single girl out of hundreds more,
supposed to make it on the USA softball team? The USA softball team
will always be a dream but being the first girl in the MLB will be my reality.
Being an MLB third baseman will fulfill my dreams.
Being an MLB third baseman will prove my brother wrong.
Being an MLB third baseman will make me proud of who I have become.
Being an MLB third baseman will make me overjoyed.
Hearing the crowds roar my name, hitting the ball over the wall in Yankee Stadium,
throwing a runner out at first, making a diving catch, seeing my name
appear on the top 10, this will make me happy, this will fulfill my dreams.
Some will tell me I'm not good enough, but I think I will succeed.
People might not believe in me but I have family and friends behind me.
Being in the MLB will mean that my years of softball will do some good for me.
Standing in the stadium with the crowd cheering my name,
I will think of that time when I first started and thank God for that day.

Lovely Days
by Campbell DiCarlo

I love the spring always
The flowers blooming bright
It bares such lovely days
They play with the wind all night
The flowers blooming bright
Spreading joy all through the day
They play with the wind all night
In the most beguiling way
Spreading joy all through the day
Trees bursting with jaunty colors
In the most beguiling way
A little bird, she flutters
Trees burst with jaunty colors
It is warm through the season
A little bird, she flutters
That is just one reason
It is warm throughout the season
It bares such lovely days
That is just one reason
I love spring always

Growing Older
by Allegria Wahle

I started off young, so free spirited, I then started going to school with so much joy
But after many years, I became too annoyed
Soon off to college, scared for my life, little did I know it would be a delight
After many years, I found the one, with whom I would spend my life
So that means a new life had begun
Many years of being together, soon later it would become dreary weather
She would die at old age, so the rest of my days I spent life in a cage
Day after day, I'm getting weaker; just waiting at home for the Grim Reaper
Just waiting at home, counting down the days
looking at all the memories in this house that will hopefully stay
I turn my head to see a picture on the wall,
of a perfectly beautiful woman, more beautiful than them all
It was of the person whom I dearly love;
hope to see her somewhere, somewhere up above
Right next to the picture, I see a clock with the time
I remember that I was counting down the hours till my bedtime
Hopefully the day will come soon, put me out of my misery
I hope to live a long-lasting life, that will go down in history
Finally that day has come to me, now to spend the rest of my days ever after happily

His Lace
by Zach Joiner

Just before Trace began to tie his shoelace
Next thing you know he was falling on his face
He was struggling to get back up
His friends walked by and said "'Sup."
This situation was a very bad case.

Generations
by Megan Barnes

It's strange to think that some day soon
we'll be in the sky like a blue balloon.
Out with the old and in with the new,
Generations before us wouldn't have a clue.
The future holds wonderful things
But now we wait for what it brings.
It's funny to think that generations from now
Will be inventing things we'd never think how.
Flying cars and springy shoes
Generations of ideas that we'll someday lose
People forgetting what was in the past
And wondering why time goes so fast.
In the end we'll always know
That generations will continue to grow.

Fall In Love With Fall
by Tori Gray

This is the time of the year called autumn or fall,
Listen in to the migrating birds
Hear their screeching calls,
Birds flying everywhere from west, east, north, or south
Along with the windy white wind ...
The weather in the fall will never be in drought
The leaves changing hues are the most beautiful things too,
In the fall it'll never be dreary or blue
With fall's crisp air
And the nice breeze that will blow in your hair
I hereby declare
That fall is the most beautiful and favorite time of the year I share,
You will love dressing head to toe in comfy clothes
And even in the fall you will look as pretty as a primrose
I suppose ...
As you sit near a cozy fire
Fall is the type of season that will never expire

Somewhere Out There
by Wesley Bryant

Somewhere out there
Is someone, something
Yearning and searching
And eternally hurting
Hoping to find that one magical thing
The thing that will one day bring
Them closer to their hopes and dreams
If only they could vividly see
What they will truly amount to be
With you and with me
We can be that one true friend
That shows them where they can begin
To be the person that makes their day
We can teach them how to believe
So they can once and for all achieve
And be someone who is forever remembered
A truly astounding society member
We need to always serve one another
So it's only fair
If we're doing something, somewhere out there

Dust and Ashes
by Eric Fotang, Jr.

The forgotten corpses that built up a castle.
The blood and bones that helped a nation ascend.
The skulls and souls grinded to push our "paradise" forward.
The bleeding hearts squashed for progress.
And the graves demolished to pave new roads.
There has been no conquest without blood shed.
There cannot be mountains without valleys.
There is no light without shadows.
There cannot be a summer without a winter.
And there is no such thing as change without a storm.
Remember, those who traded blades for us.
Remember, those chained by us.
Remember, those manipulated by us.
Remember, those murdered by us.
And remember those who wanted, those who wanted to befriend us.
Don't let them be forgotten any longer.
Don't let their skulls fade away.
Don't let them stay as stepping stone white stars resting on a sea of blue waves
splashing on a white battlefield splattered with their red blood.
Don't let their legacy stay as dust and ashes.

Fiery Love
by Mariah Davis

I want to love, I want to rekindle that flame.
Light the fire of passion. I want to long for that kiss.
But forces of nature, of people and places, want me to let go.
Run, run from your longed touch.
So I set you free, my love bird.
My passion fire.
My sweet loved kiss.

Only 4 the Righteous
by Michael A. Johnson, Jr.

"CHILL" is a word I like to use
"ABUSE" is something I've never been accused of
"LYRIC" full of truth and understanding
"HOBBIES" football, rapping and playing Madden
"SOMETHING" I've never heard is you the man bro
I'm always hearing "thank you" from my "woes"
Running through the six with my bros, feeling sorrows
"THERE IS" gonna be some trouble
"IF" we don't fix this man.
"POEMS" used for this competition and everyday life
"AGAIN" gotta make another poem so I can win this twice …

Life Means Change
by Jordan Edwards

When the sun comes up to rise
When the birds awaken
And suddenly your life is full of lies
The feeling that your soul has been taken
You think you've already won the prize
Everything is upside down
You think you've just gotten confused
You then find the urge to frown
And realize maybe everyone is connected like a fuse
Your life can't always stay the same
Through the good and the worse
You can't always have someone to blame
Everyone's life is more than just a curse
Soon the fairest of them all is destined to fall
When greatness comes with a range
Then the weakest will earn it all
And although it may sound strange
Life means change

Mi Manzana
by Chance Crigler

Mi manzana,
Mi manzana es el futuro.
Es el mañana,
tiene los sueños del nundo.
Para terminar hombre
en el hombre,
Es mi manzana.

Slip Away
by Gordon Tenev

Everywhere I gaze
Kingdoms fall
Nothing at all
Remains
Distressed yet amazed
I try to grope
On all the hope
I can contain
Foolish am I
The works of man
Will never stand
Forever
And once they die
What am I?
If all my worth's supply
Comes from such mortal endeavors?
Let my eyes gaze on someplace else

Fall Is ...
by Trinity Powell

Fall is a wonderful time of the year
When everything in your mind is so clear
Fall is a time to prepare for winter
And enjoy your family during a great Thanksgiving dinner
Fall is when you hear the cracking noise of leaves
And realize the loss of color from the trees
Fall is a time of calming relief
And enjoying God's creation of a simple beautiful leaf
Fall is when you hear birds chirping in the distance
And noise indicating other creatures' existence
Fall is a season where there is a cool and gentle breeze
And you see the wavy branches on trees

Walls
by Heather Vincent

Curly blond locks, a face hides.
Shimmering ocean eyes, hidden by a glass disguise.
Baggy clothing, so you don't know.
How big is the heart, will it ever show.
Black like the night, she wears her clothes.
Mistakes are made, she is accused.
Innocent lies beneath, the cold stone walls.
Always wronged, till the dawn comes.
Older she grows, no one stops to know.
For these walls, don't stop their growth.

What Is Fall?
by Alexis Winston

Fall is a season where leaves begin to change.
The leaves will begin to fall and hit the ground with a bang.
If you step on them now they are easily crushed.
People say it's too hot, so fall is what they rush.
Shorts and sandals are now a hoot,
It's now a time for jeans and boots.
You can see a difference when the seasons change to fall,
Now it's time to go shopping at the mall

The Food Court Adventure
by Abigail Ventimiglia

When the monster arrived at the great mall,
He felt unusually, quite small,
People were bustling about to and fro,
Mr. Fluffugous was scared and wanted to go.
But then a delicious smell crept into the air,
and his doubts vanished without a single care,
He sniffed and snorted and with a crazed bolt,
He followed the smell, and came to an abrupt halt,
in front of a glowing, yellow sign that pronounced "Food Court"
There were burgers and fries,
There were crunchy forks and knives,
There were pickles, cake, and even a fish shake!
Mr. Flufflugous looked around,
nothing he wouldn't eat to be found
and so, with a great roar,
he started consuming every food store.
With a great grin,
he was happy, no longer too thin.

Soccer
by Cassie Gomez

Soccer is a joyful sport to play.
I know you would love to feel the wind blow through your hair.
I surely do.
You feel the breeze chase you as you run across the field.
You can feel the joy that drips off your face.
Soccer is the sport you need to play because it is the sport you deserve.

His Dreams Live On
by AJ Palmer

Today is a day we all sing
In honor of Dr. Martin Luther King
Whenever people fight to be free
His name is honored in dignity
When black people weren't treated right
You were sure to hear Martin leading the fight
He fought with a love and passion, not guns or darts
He changed people's minds and hearts
But some people didn't like his words
He was taken away to a better world
Still his dream lives on that all can be free
When we knock down walls between you and me
Martin Luther King's life went by fast
But his dreams and his spirit are free at last
All because he had a dream

Camping Joys
by Isaiah Brunson

The beautiful stars in the sky
The campfire shining bright
The joyful songs, the great moods
Fireflies shining bright
Joyful moods everywhere
Kids playing hide and seek
Making sure each other does not peek
Families finally reunited
Having great dinners with each other
Learning more about one another
Telling the ups and downs of our lives
Making s'mores and creating campfire stories
Making great family memories
Until we meet again

Worry
by Hailey Duke

I worry because,
Look around.
Look at who's running for office.
Look at the sickness and poverty.
Look at the war,
Look at the hate that we have for one another.
People say, "You're too young to worry about things like that."
But I can promise you that every person my age worries
About the world that's going to be theirs one day.
We just know how to hide it,
because we don't want you to
worry.

Not What I Thought ...
by Kyla Lynch

"The box. The door. The crumbling brick. It begged me to enter ..."
I went to open the door, on the other side
It had a life I always wanted
As I lived the life I always wanted
I realized ... I don't want it at all.
Any of it ... I was given my screwed-up broken life for a reason.
To grow stronger. And prove everyone wrong.

War Grounds
by Derek Melendez

Hello me, meet the real me
I have a boot that will give you a black tooth grin
You just thinking it's my fault
But I have fire that will make you dead
Running into the depth
My head is turning into sweat
Time stand still
No one leaves and no one will
they see the strength
they getting well
but this can't save them from coming out of my hell
Now there is a war inside my head
It's time to stop
You're giving me a migraine headache
I'm leaving now, goodbye
- Inspired by "Sweating Bullets" by Megadeth,
and "Welcome Home (Sanitarium)" by Metallica

Chase
by Dorothy Boswell

It's chasing oh so quickly now, I cannot see its face.
It's getting much much closer, what a horror of a race
I'm running out of air to breathe, it's so full of hate.
I cannot find a way out, will I ever be truly safe?
I shoot up out of bed, it eases my fearful heart.
I'm thankful for what it's done, it has done its part.
I drift back into sleep, it just sits there waiting.
I think I'm glad I never knew, that it was the thing chasing.

Convicted Because of My Skin Color
by Kennedy Deveaux

Living in a world where skin color was and always will be my crime.
It's hard to believe the fact that I am discriminated
based upon the color of my skin.
Even today we still must pay for our 'crime'.
My question will always be 'why us'?
Why were our ancestors forced to work, sit in the back of the bus and be beaten.
Nowadays we still face brutality out among the streets.
Law enforcement instructs us not to resist,
even if we don't they still cuff our wrists, beat us down and shoot us dead.
Now there are many of our fellow people dead,
worthless reasons of why their blood was shed.

About Me
by Christian Ato

I am a young, intelligent man who will be attending high school.
I am a future manga artist who is going to live in Japan in the near future.
I love anime and I would love to learn how to make an anime.
I love reading stories and I love hearing telling tales.
I am a student at middle school.
I am going to be someone's inspiration someday very soon,
and I do mean very soon.
Someday I will be a person who will become very famous
in Japan for my manga series. I am going to be rich.
I want to buy my mom a house and anything else she will need,
I just want to help her.
I am a man with as much potential as the next guy
but I will use mine to get somewhere in life.
I have realized from the age of 11 what life means, or what I think it means.
Life is not about the destination but it is about making friends
along the way to the destination, which is what I believe life means.
That is all I have to say about me!

Me and My Shadow
by Dora Rice

My shadow wears crazy floral crop tops, black and white hip hop joggers
flashy Adidas originals
She knows the order of things
Her hair is like Brazilian weave
My shadow is an expression of urban fashion
Flashy, cool, and comfortable able to turn up
Able to set my passion for dance free

Heart Raised At Dawn
by Diyorahon Rakhimova

I was damned, a devil's child they told me,
And not one soul ever looked at me with even the least hint of a bit of pity.
The harshness of society and reputation shadowed around,
Wrapping itself in midnight veils and strings around myself in the soul.
My freedom was lost to it, for I was nothing
But a beast following its master's orders.
All my passion had become buried so deep that I could no longer retrieve them.
Strictness was laid upon me each day and night,
Cracking hard with the pain like in a force of a whip, both mentally and physically.
All the colors I had seen when I was younger were no longer visible,
Only blurs of ebony and stark white mixed to a fogged grey
In which was never to be returned.
The sounds I heard were no longer the music
Of when I heard the pure beauty of the violin played.
'Twas merely only just the monotone lifeless voices
Without a single trace of emotion, nor did I have any.
All my senses were dimmed and only depression and despair
Kept me from losing it all to the dark oblivion of nothing.
One night I wasn't able to hold in the torture for a moment longer,
So I had gone inside the forest, and there I wept.
Quivering, I revealed under my worn cloak a silver dagger
That could pierce a girl's heart with one blow; just like mine.
I sighed once … twice … and finally I placed the knife just below my chest,
Straight at the core of my heart. Closing my eyes, I felt the moisture on my cheek
As a crystalline teardrop fell, and I brought it at full force into my flesh.
I had reopened my eyes expecting to see blood, but to my horror
It wasn't from my chest but from my savior's arm.
Realizing what I had done, all I could do was hang my head limply
With my knees fallen with grief driven by guilt.
"Please forgive me," I cried, expecting a beating, but to my shock
He gave a warm embrace with the words, "Of course."
It was dawn but I felt so alive, and that day I learned that even if people hate you
There will always be one who doesn't.

Achieving
by Jackson Peoples

As I sit in class my mind starts to wander
Who I am, I ponder.
Today is the day I will change my mind
I don't want to get left behind.
I have many goals I hope to achieve
I just know I have to believe.
Working towards your goals is stressful
But I know in the end I will be successful.
So today is the beginning of a new day
And tomorrow I will be well on my way.

In Our World
by Lillian Piotrowski

In the forest,
There are people singing a chorus
For all the glowing eyes.
In your heart,
There's an isle of flightless birds
That have forgotten their words.
In my mind,
We have guns for hands
Contemplating out our thoughts.
In my mind's imagination,
I'm a goner
But with you together.

What If Love Exists
by Morgan Cannon

What if I'm scared?
Would you still help me through dark times?
What if I'm damaged?
Would you help repair me?
What if I'm scared of losing you?
Would you leave me anyway?
What if I told you my darkest secret?
Would you still be there for me?
What if I love you?
Would you love me back?
Now that you know my secret
What do I do?
Secrets still live on, love still exists
So what can't I seem to find it?

Magical Kingdom
by Emory Layne

A magical monorail opens the realm
fairies, princesses, pirates, rocket ships
candy shops, ice cream bars, Dole Whip, apple brew
Space Mountain, Dwarves Mine, Big Thunder Railroad
Children with shouts of glee
Those older in age make memories to be
The house of the mouse stands testament to all
The spirit of a child will always stand tall

Perspective
by Madison Miller

Perspective is everything
A small blue dot or the planet Earth
A breadcrumb or meal for an ant
A line on a map or 10,000 miles
Picking up a piece of trash or saving a life
Perspective changes everything
Is the sun colossal?
Is a skyscraper high-reaching?
Is a grain of sand just a speck?
Is a bug miniscule?
Compare
Is it really massive?
Does it really scrape the sky?
Is it really just a granule?
Is it really diminutive?
Perspective is everything

The Shadow
by Lathan Johnson

He follows me every day, every day until the sun is away
he won't leave me alone, like an ongoing song
He doesn't talk, he just stays on the sidewalk
he always lies in a straight up stare daze
Sometimes I think he's just my reflection
because he's always walking in the same direction
when the sun goes down he goes away
he goes away to where the shadows play
The next morning when the sun comes up
he starts to follow like a baby duck
he doesn't bother he doesn't speak
he only follows until the day is weak

Lyman Hall
by Madison Davis

Lyman
Trustworthy, brave, intelligent, book-worthy
John and Mary Hall
Practice medicine, preach God's word
Sadness, happiness, fear
The war, losing his wife, death
Clergyman (priest/minister), practiced medicine,
signed Declaration of Independence
To see the war be over, to live in peace
Connecticut
Hall

So Long
by Gabriel Charles

So long Earth!
Bet you thought I would never leave,
But believe me, it has not been a breeze.
So good luck old chap,
It has been fun,
Thank you for all you have done,
So long humans!
Finally, at last, my life is done.
I thought the day would never come.
Time to meet my maker!
The almighty Creator!

I Hate You
by Savannah Schofield

I hate you.
I hate how your eyes shine more green any emerald.
I hate how your voice is smoother than honey.
I hate how your arms try to draw out my fears.
I hate how you make it hard for me to breathe.
I hate how much I love you.
I love you.
I love you.
I love how your eyes gleam like a sharpened blade.
I love how your voice drips with silent malice.
I love how your pale skin tints red with thorned roses.
I love how I make it hard for you to breathe.
I love how much I hate you.
I hate you.

Forever
by Ellie McGinnis

Everything a blur.
Mascara running,
Black worn,
Hearts hurt.
A light for many, snuffed out.
Everywhere I went, I saw her.
Games we played,
Joy we made,
Coffin she lay.
Our past was a dream.
A perfect, blissful dream.
Without her, nothing.
For what is a house without its foundation?
Nothing.
I see nothing,
Feel nothing,
Love nothing.
The only thing left is the ring.
The ring that started our forever.
Why was our forever so short?

Never Escape ...
by Aria Hughes

Constantly being judged because of the color of my skin
Doubted, untrusted, and feared
Constantly being blamed, or wrongly put to trial
When asked our side of the story do you really care? Or do you think we did it?
Blamed for things way beyond what can even be left to the imagination
Unjust and unfair laws that we get blamed for.
I am black and I am proud, but are you proud
to be able to sit by me on the bus or in class?
Is it an act? Or do you really care?
Love
That is all this world needs ... One word, four letters
Love for all colors
I refuse to be known as that girl over there.
The one that is constantly being blamed for the unimaginable.
I made my own name for myself ... Aria
Ok, I am African American, but aren't I also a person
I have marrow in my bones and my heart pumps blood just like yours
I have skin no matter what color, shade, or pigment it is and so do you
I have two eyes, one nose, two hands, and two feet
But does that matter to you?

Watch Yourself
by Morgan Koehler

I may not speak
but that doesn't mean I'm not smart
I'm not skinny
but that doesn't mean I'm not beautiful
I can smile all I want
but that doesn't mean I'm happy
I dressed nice today
but that doesn't mean I'm trying to impress someone
I like to wear makeup
but that doesn't mean I'm fake
I ate a salad today
but I'm not trying to starve myself
I talked to more than one guy today
but I'm not promiscuous
I hugged my girl best friend
but that doesn't mean I'm a lesbian
Don't judge me too soon
because you may have seen me
but eyes can be deceiving.

The Little Girl
by Sadee Sherrick

A little girl sat alone,
She wept and cried,
She wanted a home,
She saw so many other kids,
They were happy, unlike her,
Happy. Smiling. Without any fear.
She wanted to be wanted,
To feel like people cared
She sat and waited for someone to come
And pick her to be their little one
She had been here for quite some time
Never chosen, it felt like a lifetime
She was waiting for a loving family to claim her as their own
Since hers has passed, gone, left her alone
Her shy eyes and faint smile told the story
Of how they were gone and not right here
All she wanted was to smile
She thought to herself, keep your head high
It won't last forever, there's always a reason why

Funerals
by Haven Warner

Funerals
Caskets, death
Crying, weeping, sobbing
Mascara down girls' faces
Sorrow, black, heart attack
Preachers, family
Love

The World of a Shadow
by Garrett Miller

The world of a shadow isn't that different you see,
All the people are cast from your feet,
And everything you see on the land,
Is cast on the floor where you stand,
They hide from the sun so they don't burn,
That is one thing they always learn,
The life of a shadow starts when you're born,
And stays with you so you won't be forlorn,
And when you are dead,
the shadow will bow its head,
and cry,
And will lie down with you in the pine box you lie.

Past and Future
by Sidney P. Moore

I was born in 2003
My mother and father took care of me
I had troubles in elementary school
The other students thought I was a fool
Fast-forward a few years
While I was in school I had a lot of fears
In the 4th grade it was unbearable of how many conflicts I got in
Then my mother said, "Now that's enough"
She transferred me to another school to teach me the right stuff
I was at that school for a year
And I had no fear
Now I'm in my new academy
Now my mother can be even more of me
I have been here for three years now
When I look at my past I just say, "Wow"
Also I have been getting good grades this year
And guess what, I have NO FEAR

And Then You've Grown Up
by Mina Amirkhani

And then you've grown up.
When there's no time to go out and play,
When going to sleep early is good,
Everybody expects you to say,
The things you should.
When you start to call your parents now,
And tear the posters off the wall,
You begin to wonder how,
This happened at all.
Your first job is a blessing in disguise,
And you think it's a piece of cake,
However, it has been far too idealized,
Your image was a fake.
The day comes to an end,
An expected one too,
Family gathers around all for you.
Hear them talk all about your life
From beginning to end.
Your successes and failures seem to suffice,
As you begin to ascend.

The Day We Meet Again
by Daniela Borda

Time goes by quick like a jet
But I hope I can still see you once again.
Yet I am different now
By the time you see me you will say wow.
I hope you've changed too
But not like face one or face two.
When we see each other I will greet you with a smile
Because I haven't seen you in a while.
We will run and we will play
Like the old times back in the day.
To cheer you up when things are gone
To make you giggle with the show called "The Wiggles"
To make you laugh like a crazy giraffe.
I will show you my life
And everything will be right
Just know that I am here
And there won't be any tears.
Friends we must stay
Or all of our adventures will go away
But know that I am here waiting for that day.

December 25
by Eziada Ezinwa-Ezuma

Music, music songs of joy,
Songs of pleasure that won't annoy.
Lights and stars upon the tree,
Shine above for you and me.
But Christmas isn't about these things,
It's about our Savior, the newborn King!
So join with joy, as we say Merry Christmas,
For Christ is the reason we celebrate this.

Growing Old
by Jourdan Crocker

What is growing old?
Is it the feeling of being cold
Does it happen quick like mold
What is it?
Is it a sad feeling
Or is it the feeling when you walked for a while, then sat down
Is it a happy feeling
Or is it the feeling when you've lost someone you loved
Is it a good feeling
Or the feeling of being unloved
What is growing old, and what is being loved?

ABC
by Erica Walker

A, B, C
1, 2, 3
How long will they be with me
As our futures go on
And we start to grow and learn
And stories are uncovered about all we didn't know, and all we must earn
A, B, C
Doe, Ray, Me
What if I press the wrong note and get off-key?
Will they simply turn their backs and abandon me
Or will they say it's all okay and we'll sing together and they'll stay
A, B, C
Please stay with me
As our roads slowly separate from each other
Just tell me that we'll always be together
Although I know this won't last forever ...

Wasted Time
by Addi Neumann

Broken glass
broken plates
if you mess with me
I'll break your face.
Broken hearts
Wasted time
You left me in such little time.
I hate you, you hate me
let's just forget all our memories.

Our World
by Breanna Thompson

This world is sick and cruel, people are always breaking rules.
We lie, and cheat, and think it's neat, but instead we end up in juvie.
We say we'll change, but we stay the same,
We make fun of people because of their weight.
We hang with crowds that bring us down, because of this we act out.
We shun the light, but let in the dark, we have horrible, cold, evil hearts.
We say we're okay we're not afraid, we try to be brave, but we fall on our face.
We all mess up and make mistakes, but for Heaven's sake,
Please have hope and pray.

The Pale Blue Dot
by Sebastian Elisan

That pale blue dot is not a lot
From a view in space, it is just a spot.
But it is our home,
Where we can roam.
It is our Earth;
And it's holding all our worth
Yet people all the same,
Are fighting with no aim.
We can treat our planet better
It deserves a thank you letter
We should cherish our chance
Our one-in-a-million chance
That our Earth has the right conditions
To let us stand in our positions
That we are in today.
Earth will never betray
It's the only home we know
That we shouldn't overthrow

Softball
by Shelby Rooker

Under the stars, under the lights
On the field using all my might
On the field, ready to hit
I really hope I do not miss
In the stands, I hear my name
As I take my swing, I hear the ball making a ding
Around first I go, as I go to second
I knew, I could make it
I get to third knowing I can go
When I get home I hear my team shout
Home run, we're winning tonight

Grandparents
by Madison Tucker

Going to my grandparents can be such fun
My grandma and I just walking but more talking
They've time to wipe a tear, they are wonderful through the year
They make me laugh with such joy
Their love is like a little dove
To be in their warmth and know that you are loved
They sing and dance with all their hearts
The little creative things they make me enjoy their smarts
They are wise, they also cry
I look up to them and I know that I can be like them
I can learn to cook, I can also learn to hit the books
They are special to me

The Noise
by Makuyan Walker

As I walked to my door,
There were loud noises and something fell on the floor.
Once I went inside; there was no one in sight,
And I was starting to be filled with fright.
There was a loud strike and a flash of light.
The house was no longer bright.
I could see nothing in sight,
But I had a feeling everything would be alright.
As I continued walking,
I heard a sound of something knocking.
When I turned around, there was nothing.
The thought that there was nothing,
It still felt really haunting.

Breathe In, Breathe Out
by Ashanti Rice

Breathe in fighting
Breathe out standing up for others
Breathe in stealing
Breathe out asking for it
Breathe in war
Breathe out having peace
Breathe in violence
Breathe out communicating
Breathe in calling people names
Breathe out being respectful
Breathe in hating people
Breathe out loving one another
Breathe in being messy
Breathe out smiling
Breathe in disrespect
Breathe out family
Breathe in cussing
Breathe out consequences
Breathe in bullying
Breathe out getting suspended

Undersea Gala
by Eden Dyer

Up on land, a peaceful velvet sky sparkled with rhinestone stars,
Foam crashed salt-bleached driftwood against the beach's sandy bars,
But underneath the purple sky and the choppy sapphire waves,
A lavish, aquatic ball was beginning to take place.
One by one the fish filed in, their frilly fins dripping with jewels,
Their Technicolor scales glistened in the reflective light of the pool.
The ladies in their poofy ball dresses sewn from satiny kelp,
The gentlemen in their crisp tuxedos offering a fin to help.
The grand hall was hung with garlands of bubbles, chandeliers of pearls, too.
With stained sea-glass windows and velvet sofas, a deep ocean blue,
Glittering seashell chairs were resting around the room,
And anglers' lamps illuminated the otherwise gloom.
As the starfish orchestra opened the night with a bright and rousing tune,
The fish paired off into couples, sailing across the room.
Do-si-dos and tangos, jigs and arabesques,
Bubbles of exhaustion flowed freely by the time they took a rest.
Next refreshments of fruit punch and sea pigs in a blanket were served,
A basic round of hors d'oeuvres before the main course.
And afterwards the party guests, plump and refreshed,
Bid their partners adieu, and exited for a rest.

What Is Life
by Briana Pierre

Is it a blessing from Heaven, or a curse from Earth
Is it a long happy journey, or a trial from birth
Is it something that you're thankful for, or something that you hate
Is it a rain of happiness, or hail on your parade
Is it full of laughter and smiles, or something not worthwhile
Is it a never-ending disgrace, or a long race with a slow pace
Whatever life is to you, it's a great experience so take it
Whether this is false or true, life is what you make it

The Wolf's Chase
by Symira Brown

As I sniff the air, I smell my prey
I am hidden in the shadows but my eyes are bright as day
Oblivious to the predator, my prey continues to eat
I cautiously begin to stealthily move my feet
I move with caution, trying not to make a sound
I step on a twig, when my paw hits the ground
It was already too late, my prey began to run
I growl out in anger, eyes blazing like the sun
I chase my prey and catch the little beast
I howl in victory as to now I will feast

A Pale Blue Dot
by Tanner Fink

Just a dot in space
Just a spot containing the human race
It looks like nothing
It's just a nihility
But really it's something
With supreme ability
Everyone who was
Everyone who would
Everyone who has
Everyone who could
All living things have walked this planet
Like kings who stood upon the granite
Not just a dot
So next time don't take it for granted
Not just a spot
Our little blue planet

Illusionary Love
by Annie Roberts

As my eyes caught a sight that looked to be shining bright
I was caught in the moment and was trapped inside.
Chasing a mirage that I could not believe was true
When it vanished away I could feel my heart break.
Now all I hear is the echo of your voice
Remembering all the things you said and things we had planned to do.
Maybe I was just the one that was blinded by everything
No, we were just desperate for the thing that was called love
Now your warmth that I hold
Will soon be forgotten and will go cold
And I fear it will feel like you were never here at all.
Deep down we knew that this illusion would never last
But no matter what they said, no matter what we said
I still thought we could have a happy future ahead.
Friendly mornings bring a new day and lonely nights are swept away
One day someone new will paint me in their own way.
And the warmth that we shared will be lost in the air.
With these memories finally being laid to rest.

The Spanish Swordsman
by Nathan Davenport

Skilled sword-work is written on his hands, delicate yet firm.
His fingers are long and slender, with years of constant swordplay perfected.
These scar-worn hands firmly grip a hilt of brass
With guard of gold, embroidered.
Rapiers are drawn as two men, like whirlwinds, collide
With the clash of blades,
Steel on steel resounding.
This place of battle, where swords cross, is rough,
Where stone and sand meet with a fortress,
Dilapidated, and without inhabitant, save those few who live and die by sword.
This stronghold is besieged on one side by a deadly fall,
Deep into a hungry tide
That licks its chops in rhythm with the stones that fall to its depths.
Near the cliff edge stands the opponent,
Right handed, yet with left, his rapier has drawn.
Clothed in black, with colorless mask, he interrogates:
"Who are you, and what are your intentions?"
The reply comes quickly: "I am Inigo Montoya and I seek my father's murderer."
-Quote based upon the character, Inigo Montoya, from "The Princess Bride"

Ode To Death
by Aaron Milligan

The difference between death
and life in the living,
Doesn't lie in the body but the soul
and the place that it's risen.
But one can't deny the knowing hunger of death
as it creeps and tries to take over,
The distant in the existent,
And the peace in a corpse,
Can't remove us from this dead high horse.
It hangs like an apple,
Taunting your life.
"Come I know you wanna take a bite."
Its secrets and lies that it ties to disguise,
will bring with your bite total demise.
So cherish the life with all that is given,
So when the knock comes you know you've liven.
And death won't bite or bring its sting,
Because you will be an eternal being.

Night and Day
by Ivan Budanov

An indignant staccato, a dragon's breath,
A shiver in a cold January morning,
A vase of bright roses, a vase of dead roses,
Crescendo, decrescendo, emotion to emotion,
Sprinting to Mendelssohn's March,
Sobbing to La Traviata.
The limitless sky, the open bottle, the soft kiss.
The soft slap.
Waking up, sore head, light smile,
Warm sun, cold moon,
Again, and again, and again.
140 in the Autobahn, zooming through life,
After 50, it goes by pretty fast, life.
Itchy cashmere, crumpled cinnamon.
A lackluster past, present, future,
But still, the bright sun gleams out on us,
And the beat of a drum,
Is enough to make people dance and love.

Laughter
by Claire LaRose

Laughter, something everyone loves,
The sound of it
The smile on someone's face when you see it
Something that could make your day
Or give you a lifelong memory
The bond it might create
With someone who relates
Love and friendship
Hope to get through a bad day
Laughing is the cure,
It's magical
Laughter, is the right medicine any day, every day

Calories
by Shelby Rewis

Raw steaks are red, blueberries are blue
Candy is sweet and so is food
Hamburgers are life, like chicken fried rice
Makes my mouth water but it costs more than a quarter
Lattes, which are always pumpkin spice
I never get ice, wonderful scent of cinnamon
Barely gripping my cup, it's so warm
This coffee is kicking in
Waking up to the sound of popping grease
Quickly extending my hand and saying, "Please?"
Bacon, eggs, toast oh my!
Now that I've gotten plump, time for me to say goodbye.

The Game Winner
by Zavian Thomas

The sounds of the cheering fans sounded like a roaring sea
As the linebacker intercepted the ball, he jetted down the field with glee
Getting to the end zone he knew they would win
All he had to do was make it 90 yards in.
He shuffled down the field breaking through opponents as if he was made of steel
Kicking away opponents as they were snapping at his heel
Now at the 40 on the opponent's territory, all there is left is an open field to score
As the linebacker reached the end zone the fans' cheering turned into a loud uproar
The game is finished with the score 32-26
Coaches and players ran on the field to congratulate the linebacker for the pick six
As for the losers, they walked off the field with their heads down
All players and coaches left with a frown.

Escape From the Monochrome World
by Aamina Dhar

A monochrome world we live in,
"Look at the color," they all say.
Their clock-like hearts beat beneath sallow skin,
While I drowned in unshed tears and my tenuous heart decayed.
Vacuous ideals hurled at me,
And in horror I turned to flee.
But all around me they grinned,
And left without option, I turned within.
At first the caliginous, satin ribbon choked me.
My tears cascaded down my cheeks until the darkness set me free.
It unfurled a path, speechlessly I ambled down,
My footsteps making vestal notes; my thoughts became my crown.
The mellow notes underfoot wove their songs into color,
And the black satin bloomed into an iridescent world with a shudder.
The whip of oppression and the drug of depression no longer rent my heart,
For the now the colors and sounds have secrets to impart.

The Need For Greed
by Nikolas Struntz

You aspire to be different, to be superior.
You desire success, but success is never enough.
You strive for unreachable perfection, demanding improvement.
The nature of greed is the nature to be different, to be better.
You long for authority,
To have power, wealth, influence, respect, and to be in control.
You want to affect the world in your way.
You yearn for greater intellect,
To be quick-witted, intuitive, imaginative, and academically competent.
You want to comprehend the world around you.
You feel the need to fit in,
To be popular, acknowledged, socially inclined, and distinguished.
You want to be well-known, you want to be talked about.
You want to make a difference,
But you feel powerless, unworthy, disrespected, and inadequate.
You say you can't, and I ask why not, simply because you can.
You want to be someone else,
Someone who is content with being themself.
This person is nonexistent,
Greed fuels constant improvement, it fuels the necessary desire to change.

The Color of Life
by Jamian Jackson

If my life was a color it would be gray
Something so simple like night and day
When I am down my thoughts stand still
Like the money in my wallet, a dollar bill
Sometimes I wonder what life would be like
To be someone else, play baseball, get a strike
Those thoughts can be there for a while
But still I would like to smile
Being gloomy is bad for man
Just let flow, the water out of the dam
If my life was a color it would be blue
Look for a new future, how about you

Fast 'N' Loud
by Joshua Clardy

The deep rumble of the exhaust
contrasts with the elegant and soft
nature, in which we were taught.
The power of the modern motor
is comparable to that of solar
and everyone knows the unique odor.
The brand new beautiful paint
where there is no taint
the one piece of the car in which there is no complaint.
Although they look like they are from Mars
I challenge you to look to the stars
and think of a world without cars.

My Grandma
by Cayla Bias

My grandma always knits me sweaters
Her sweaters always make me feel better
My grandma is very nice and sweet
She always bakes me tasty treats
My grandma takes me to many different places
Wherever we go I see many different faces
My grandma treats me with a lot of love
My grandma is as elegant as a dove
My grandma is a person that likes to share
My grandma treats everyone with care
My grandma is very good friend
The friendship between my grandma and I will never end

Thoughts In an Instant
by Hannah Korn

Motion has stopped
Everything at a standstill
Even clocks don't tick.
Choices, choices gone
All the possibilities,
Stopped in their tracks.
No time keeps going
The tidal waves that push, pull
The Earth stops spinning.
Yet I keep walking
Somehow I can go onward
Down the long, dull streets.
Through my eyes I see,
Through my ears I hear too much,
But no one else does.
Frozen is my world
I feel doomed to walk on but,
Just for an instant.

Forgotten
by Marisol Garcia

She is gone!
She is done!
Just because she stopped trying,
Always unknown crying.
She wishes she were perfect; she says it's not fair
When she hears people talking about her hair.
They laugh in her face,
But they haven't even tried to be in her place.
It starts with one word they blurt;
They didn't know they were her biggest fear!
Every day she awoke with regret;
All she wanted to do was forget.
All their actions caused one big scar
Which she tried to wash away without alarm.
Now she lies still.
Forgotten by will.
Her memories drowned.
Unremembered in solitary peace.

Battle Scars
by Lauren Bailey

Their eyes sunken in, their faces so pale.
They used to be strong men, now they're frail.
No legs, no arms, bleeding and scarred.
As they march in the line that uttered distress,
thinking only of the words, "Their country, they will protect."
They want us to be free, and they want to be just.
Our soldiers march on in the bloody battle dust.
Finally they approach the aim of the enemies' fire.
Some fall, some wounded, but it's still a large number.
They bravely move on like nothing had happened.
Faithfully following their gallant captain.
Our troops look around, shaken and scared,
with the echo of the bombs being prepared.
But still they fight on with such great intensity,
with the one reason, to save those back in their home cities.
These men and women sacrifice daily,
to defend a nation that is always complaining.
My only call to you, I'll keep it simple,
be aware of our troops, and always be thankful.

Categories
by Endia Dees

I fall under a category,
Which one? I'm not sure.
I've tested life without worry,
And found a cure already.
To every stressful situation,
Not every problem needs a complex equation.
Life is like rotating stations,
Sleeping and praying to be awakened.
Try as I might,
I still find myself underrated,
Yet, I am who I was created to be,
Can't hide nor fake it.
Auditioned numerous times for various situations,
To no surprise, I made it.
Focus and determination got me a place in this;
This world I'm living in,
I fall under a category,
Which one? I'm not sure.

Treason Upon the Hill
by David Sikes

I've always wondered what would happen to me
If I sat here so still
But now it is so plain to see
Whilst sitting upon this hill
Looking down it I see so clear
Trees and bees galore
There's only one thing that I fear
A pack of wild boar
I know it's odd
But there's a reason
For the will of God
I committed treason
Everyone was astonished
For what I've done
I must be punished
I cannot run

I Miss My Dad
by Alanah Cleare

I miss my dad
Every night I pray to God that he's okay.
I pray that he is safe and happy.
I miss my dad
Every night I call just to hear his voice and to imagine him being there.
I miss my dad.
Every time I see Law and Order I weep a little inside.
That was our show.
The smell of his cologne when he hugs me goodnight.
The scratchy feeling when he gives me a kiss goodbye.
I miss my dad.
My twin.
My everything.
I miss the singing.
The late night dinners.
I miss my dad.

Which One To Choose
by Caleb Germany

What color will it be?
Should it be dark or bright?
Will it be the colors of the day
Or the colors of the night?
What shape will it be?
Will it have wings?
Will its beauty make it possible
To belong to kings?
What size will it be?
Will it be big or small?
Will its face be large?
Will it be short or tall?
The thing about dragons that you should know
Before thinking about having one,
Is that they can be cool in fiction,
But dangerous in reality.
So if anything, I might rather have
A short, yet loveable dog named Rocco.

Running Away
by Lisa Prystupa

Wandering into a forest shrouded in darkness and mystery. A tiny girl I see.
Was it an illusion? But what lies beyond?
Shadowy figures and fog, frightened, shaking, scared ... gotta run!
Running and running he can move no more, oh no, no, no, he's being followed
Wandering deeper and deeper he sees spirits appearing,
appearing shapeless and hollow.
There was a girl as well who he knew from before, in another time.
Trembling and scared he thinks no! I don't want to disappear ...
I don't want to go away!
A girl he does not know says, "I'll be your friend?" Should he go?
Temptation, does he stay or do what he does not know?
Staying the path he considers wandering spirits
and what he thinks is a dark aura perceived to surround his life.
By taking this it's an easy out to what he thinks is strife.
As morning comes the spirits return to their usual selves,
wandering and running will not improve his life.
His life is not like he perceives.
He realized what he struggled with and the snow glistened in the morning light
as the birds sang their little song.
The fog is gone and the boy runs to his mom and dad
and sings a song of praise and love.

Just Because
by Quin King

Just because I'm shy
Doesn't mean I don't like you
Doesn't mean I don't want to talk to you
And doesn't mean I don't want to be friends
Just because I'm a boy
Doesn't mean I'm strong
Doesn't mean I'm brave
Doesn't mean I'm a sports lover
And doesn't mean I play sports
Just because I'm angry
Doesn't mean it's your fault
Doesn't mean that I hate you
Doesn't mean that I can't stand you
And doesn't mean we're not still friends
So why can't we be friends
Why must boys be strong and brave
When will everyone be friends

Our Life
by Brianna Henderson

Once it was a big empty ball,
Waiting to be filled with nature, love and life,
Waiting for the first stone wall,
To be put up to bear life,
Soon it begins to fill,
Adding animals and plants,
And oceans and hills,
Waiting for the laughter and dance,
Of all the wonders God creates,
Then we came,
The speck in the world everyone loved,
When in a dark place we're always the flame,
And when the time comes for us to go,
We'll leave our mark on the world,
By being the inspiration to the one who always looked up to us,
Since the day we came in so small,
To the day we went away being the biggest thing we can ever envision.

Where I'm From
by Leighton Willoughby

I am from Palm Beach, Florida,
From salty air and hibiscus flowers
I am from orange juice,
From freshly picked oranges.
I'm from surfing and beach volleyball,
From David and Stacey
I'm from "suck it up buttercup,"
And "eat all your food"
I'm from seashells
That we made into necklaces.
I'm from warm winters and tan bodies,
From wearing shorts all year,
Going to the beach,
And always being outside.
In my desk drawer are my best memories,
From birth to teen,
And kindergarten projects
I am from these memories
I am from Palm Beach, Florida

Breathe In/Breathe Out
by Emily Rutland

Breathe in everyone dies
Breathe out life is being born
Breathe in war
Breathe out love
Breathe in life without music
Breathe out piano music
Breathe in hate
Breathe out trust
Breathe in money
Breathe out tranquility
Breathe in mutes
Breathe out the ability to sing
Breathe in people dying at a young age
Breathe out being alive
Breathe in bullying
Breathe out parents who love you
Breathe in people dying in war
Breathe out they are protecting us
Breathe in we all feel pain
Breathe out we are all different

A Holding Hand
by Britney Barfield

The heart can only take so much
When it overloads it starts to clutch
You reach out, there is nobody there
You cry out, but it's too much to bear
Just take my hand I'm right here for you
No matter the extent of what you're going through
When it becomes too much just bow your head
Take a breath, He'll do what He says
There is more in front than there is behind
So, when you get down just close your eyes
Strap in for the ride and hold on tight
The good Lord is not going to sit out this fight

Beach Life
by Morgan Faith

Waves crashing on the sand, as I am getting tan
The sun is so bright and that is quite alright
Riding waves, collecting seashells and hanging ten
Ocean air, salty hair
High tides, good vibes
Vacation, relaxation
Tropical waters, sand dollars
Seagulls and seashells, palm trees and waves
Oh how I wish I was there, breathing that fresh, sun kissed ocean air.

Crayon
by Ashley Freeman

He gives color
Which turns into mood
Emotional reactions
Turn into gray at close
Never a scribble
Never a scrawl
A kind of communication tool
Always mightily crisp
Wanting to draw
Maybe it'll turn into a depiction
Like a wanted for hire sign
Desk, paper, canvas
The crayons fall
He manages to finish the drawing
Without a scribble or scrawl

Pajamas Are ...
by Erin Cofield

Pajamas are warm.
Pajamas are comfortable.
Pajamas are creative.
Pajamas are colorful.
Pajamas are fluffy.
Pajamas are good for sleeping.
Pajamas are good for reading books.
Pajamas are good for watching late night TV.
Pajamas are good for eating midnight snacks.
Pajamas are good for having sleepovers.

Laughter
by Claire Rich

Laughter
Walks around with an open hand
Waiting for someone to take it
If only someone would take a chance and change it
Dropping it off at doorsteps
Like a present waiting to be opened
Breathing fresh air
Smelling like roses
Changing a frown to a smile
Making someone's day
Laughter is worth a thousand smiles on a rainy day

Foundation of Life
by Victoria Tobias

The stars twinkle like diamonds in the night
Our dreams not willing to give up without a fight
Our hope glimmers brighter than any moon
Letting them go will certainly mean our doom
When our will is true it's stronger than any knife
Without these dreams what is the meaning of life
Without these dreams we wouldn't have the strength to go on
Before we knew it civilization would be gone
All those people we look up to right now
They managed to follow their dreams somehow
These are the people that our world knows
These are the people that choose their dreams
And through our history it beams
A lesson that makes our world strong
If you follow your dreams you can never be wrong

Alone
by Mary Grey Shaginaw

Alone. With ourselves.
Our thoughts and actions, we are alone with them.
Whatever you do, say, feel and think,
you will be alone with that for the rest of your life.
A negative thing? Maybe.
A positive thing? Most certainly.
Each and every person has a past and most people want to put that past away.
But no- it doesn't work that way.
You need to dig it up, feel everything and everything that comes with it.
Then, once you feel at peace with it, it is okay to put it away, and be alone with it.

William Du Bois
by Daisy Colquitt

William
Determined, leader, brave, courageous
Son of Mary Silvina and Alfred Du Bois
Education, writing, family, freedom
Angry, segregated, depression
Slavery, racial hatred, being segregated
Given the Lenin Peace Prize, founder of the Niagara Movement,
writer of many books and essays.
Equality, education for all people
Atlanta, Georgia
Du Bois

Giving Myself the Pain
by Savannah Guilty

I see the way you look at her, but the way you never look at me anyway.
You were the guy I was scared to open up my eyes to
because I already knew you were too broken up inside.
I was a fool to fall for you and let the tears I cry out for you
hidden in the depth of my pillow.
The sun never seem to rise when I'm not with you
or the stars never seem to shine when I'm not beside your side.
Staying away from my feeling for you and for losing myself in you
When I was never beneath, the tears in your heart made me want you more.
The feelings I had for you were too powerful to come outside
or they would burst into daylight.
In your heart you are lonely and the lights are cut off
And it's too dark that you need a flashlight.
So I became war for you that my hearts never skips a beat without you.

War
by Ethan Gallagher

We lived far out, in our own paradise
I always enjoyed home, it was pretty nice
Back in my youth, my home was Japan
But to my dismay, World War Two began
My dad left the house, the last time I've seen him
But now my whole family is gone, and I miss them
We didn't see much of the war for some time
But that changed in an instant, in 1945
A bomb was dropped, couldn't have been far away
The loudest thing I've ever heard, the noise that it made
I see in the distance, what looked like a mushroom
The smell of ash, and the feeling of doom
I don't know what I was thinking, but I started to run
I knew it was over, I think my life's done
But I just kept running as fast as I can
Away from that blast, I got out of Japan
I thought in my head, nothing gold can stay
Because everything perfect will have its day

Broken Pride
by Madison Stewman

African-American, Black, Negro
Stepped on and buried under all,
You assume I am not capable.
Think we aren't on the same level.
Am I not human?
You chained me to stereotypes,
My ancestors killed, mistreated, beaten.
Scholars broken to pieces and told they were trash.
Are we not the same?
Police are supposed to protect.
What have we done to you?
But we will not sleep,
We will not allow man to slow us down, to treat us like dirt under your feet.
I will not retaliate with your ways.
I am stronger.
We will rise.
We can love.
We can heal.
Soothe my broken pride.

Believe
by Taylor Allison

It all started back in 2009,
Now he's partnered with Calvin Klein,
He got into some trouble,
And hit the rubble,
But he got up off the ground,
And turned himself around,
Now his Beliebers are back,
And we're ready to attack,
Any haters,
Or traitors,
On Purpose Tour 2016.

Equal Rights
by Jodi Everett

Equal rights, who cares?
the people sure don't
They say equality is unfair
and change is something they want
They say equality is bad
and should be put into a corner
with all of the issues that are so sad
and without a single mourner
It is time to stand up
and forget the ones who say it's wrong
it's time to stop being trained like a pup
And speak the truth that's been hidden for so long...

Words of Money
by Allen Robertson

These words are nothing but money, this poem, a bank.
My input, nonexistent, my words: blank
I want to resist, but I fear the authority.
This school is draining my words, taking all the creativity.
This whole poem is just to make cash.
If we do not make them money, our grades they will surely bash.
This whole contest is just a money scheme,
If only we'd rebel together as a team.
I'm doomed to waste my talent, no way to free my words.
They are trapped in cages, just like birds.
This was formed because of my teacher,
And I hope this poem will teach her.

Life's Treasures
by Jordan Sul

Our world is ever changing
Through times of peace and war.
Every life is precious;
None worth less or more.
But we will not live forever,
So love them while they last.
And make the most of all your joy
For the best things die too fast.
In this age loss is inevitable
And death in the end is sure
Live your life now while you can
And love all that is pure.
Every soul has rights and wrongs
These things are beyond measure.
And even though time is too short,
Life truly is a treasure.

Internet Friends
by Bella Salvo

The internet is improving in all sorts of ways
You can make new friends in just a few days
I have internet friends
They come from all over the states
We talk and give updates
I have internet friends
Mandy, Molly, Hannah, Virginia, Lydia, Kelsey
Just to name a few
We stick together like glue
We share about our days and what we have been thorough
We are not schoolmates and we have not met
Although this does not make us upset
I have internet friends
We like to talk about what it would be like to meet
We think that we would all fall to our feet
I like to think that we would all click together
We could be friends forever
No matter wherever we are
I have internet friends

Everything Loved Withers Away
by Pranati Madala

Everything loved withers away
A dog once loved and cared
Soon goes down and forever taken away
A mother that pours love and care
Soon vacates and never returns
The things we love and the things we care
Soon taken away by the mother above
Then handed down again and again
Like the cycle of love and despair
Often given to the kids of the mother above
The mother above knows when to give and when to take
Despite the tantrums her kids make
Throughout people's lives, they all go through the cycle of love and despair
Whether wanted or not, everything loved withers away

I Am Kira Estep
by Kira Estep

I am a smart girl that wants to be a doctor
I wonder if I will make it past med school?
I hear the sounds of medical devices
I see patients getting better
I want to be the best doctor
I am a smart girl that wants to be a doctor
I pretend to be a doctor
I feel a scalpel in my hands
I touch my surgical mask and put it on
I worry I won't make it past intern year
I cry if something bad happens
I am a smart girl that wants to be a doctor
I understand how hard this journey will be
I say, "I believe God can get me through it."
I dream about being chief of General Surgery
I hope I will be the best doctor
I am a smart girl that wants to be a doctor

Four Years Old
by Michael Vining

The time has come little sis
Your birthday is finally here
Now you are three
Then you will be four.
When you were one year old
You came into this world
You came for a specific purpose
But only you can find out what it is.
Then you became two
You learned to walk
You started to talk
O you just loved to talk.
Now you are three
You started school
Now the only thing is
What happens at four

Opportunities
by Madelyn Grimes

You watch as all the citizens hustle about;
They push, shove, and yell at passersby.
A woman sits by a fence with a crying baby, a box at her feet.
A tired expression is plastered on her face as she begs for anything.
The bus pulls up and you're on your way to your new home.
Men with briefcases,
Women in clicking heels all pile on with you.
"I will succeed at this," you decide as you watch
The rude people flying past the window.
"New York University!" The driver yells out your stop.
You get up and slowly walk off.
Staring in disbelief at the huge building before you, you walk into the doors;
The doors of a new life, new opportunities.
This is your chance to reinvent yourself, to make it big.
Go for it: You won't succeed unless you try.

Friends
by Savanah Allen

Friends:
Here and there smiling and laughing
Always having pictures taken
Sleeping bags to nights in hotels
Here and there smiling and laughing
One ear bud in each girl's ear
Jumping on each other's back screaming with glee
Here and there smiling and laughing
Making friendship bracelets
Going to late night shows
Here and there smiling and laughing
Doing each other's hair and nails
Going shopping all around
Here and there smiling and laughing
In the summer swimming and splashing
In the winter skiing and bonfires
-Oh, how that will never be me

My Hatred In Heart
by Logan Swanson

As madness and hatred fills me up
Betrayed and slaughtered by those I loved
Can this be something worse
Destroyed my hope I now know force
Everything here was happy but now sad
Finding my meaning that makes me go mad
Growing in anger, pain unknown
Hell breaks loose in a fiery tone
I am a killer, murderer's king
Justice gone we're all now thieves
Killing all those who stand against me
Love no longer, what thrives only mutiny
My heart, a now cracked rock
Now gone, those who I was mocked
Open in fire I find my soul
Pandemic rampant world filled with coal
Questioning myself, wondering where it started
Rage and despair now in construction
So help me I fear my own destruction

Breathe
by Anna Tran

Do you know what you do
Even to "try-hards" and "can-do attitudes"
Boy, if you knew, it would be different
Right?
Hey, it's me, the biggest disappointment you know.
Well, sure, I try my best for you
But, you don't seem to be pleased.
Abuse me.
Leave me in my room to cry. Help.
What do you want from me?
"What a great role model you have to look up to"
What if I told them what really happens
What if I don't just sit back and say "I'm fine" this time
Would you still bruise?
I mean, where would I run off to
Hear me
Embody what love is for once
Listen
Please

Never Everlasting
by Kendall Stephens

You come in new and leave old
It was warm then gets cold
They bloom pretty and fade away
It starts shining then gets grey
Everything starts
Then breaks hearts
It rolls to an end
Sadness becomes a trend
A smile goes to a frown
And sorrow spreads all around
Laughter goes to grief
It builds up high
Turns into a lie
then comes crashing down
The beginning is one day
That is bright and cheerful with not a thought of gray
And the end is another
Happiness comes to an end, when it does it does not return

Tatum Brown

If I Were To Become a Writer
by Tatum Brown

If I were to become a writer, I'd take after the sky;
tapping deep into the night on my silver typewriter
and pasting every stray line and lyric,
every stanza and stack of dialogue,
every ellipsis,
typed thought,
dream,
every memory and punctuation mark
into a nebula of poetry
just for you
to explore with your kaleidoscope
and string my expressions of love
into
constellations.

Noordeep Kaur

Reactions
by Noordeep Kaur

THE MOTHER catches herself caressing her stomach,
and stops herself quickly,
It's a habit she's gotten used to, and it will not leave her very swiftly.
She looks around forlornly at the room she made for her,
sighing wistfully, for everything she had imagined will never occur.
Perhaps she would've been a Sophia, or maybe even a Rowan,
But now that seems like a right Death has stolen.
THE FATHER stares out the window, with a vacant, desolate stare,
eyes full of broken dreams and unwanted despair.
Without even seeing her, he has memorized her like a prayer,
And if she had decided to stay, he would've raised her with great care.
A teardrop nestles in the corner of his dull, brown eyes,
and he hopes that she knows that he will love her till the day he dies.
THE BROTHER plays quietly, with a petite doll in his hands,
even though he is lost in thought, thinking about other tempting lands.
Lands where there would've been a small girl at his side,
a girl he would've bickered with but still protected from the wild.
Everywhere he looks now, he receives looks of pity and sympathy,
And it's only because without wanting to, she decided to break their
hearts viciously. Another soul, another death, another broken family,
For Death this is a normal day, and he continues on grimly.

1st Place

Ariana Williams

Ariana is an 8th grade student
who loves green tea, cats, and rowing.
She also loves her friends, as they inspire her creativity.
As for her award winning poem, she credits a small idea,
which, like most of her work,
simply blossomed into something entirely new.
Thank you, Ariana!

She Still Has Scars
by Ariana Williams

Her tears are censored
She's frozen
Crystallized
As she hides behind her mascara
And the lies
The lies they told her
She repeats them
It's her hope
False dreams tied around her wrists
Like rope
Like rope they lead her
Leaving marks
Thin red lines
Traced around her hips and arms
Which she hides
She soothes my worry
Sisterly and brave
"I'll live. I'm here.
I'm not afraid."

Division IV

Grades
10-12

My Life
by Shantanika Sallis

My life is a whirlwind, and I keep on spinning and spinning
You have to live with being worthless
Because everyone around you is not loving
I often sit by myself and cry,
Because deep down inside, I know
No one wants to be in my life.
No one knows what it's like to be mentally abused,
But throughout this poem I will tell you.
You have to put up with being called all kinds of things, but
Eventually, you'll be set free.
My life is not all sweet and nice,
But know one thing, I'm doing just fine.
I think all of this trouble I had to go through was for the better
Because I have a God up there, and I know He's always there.
I also have a mom who loves me with all her heart,
And she even told me that we will never be apart.
My life happened to turn out pretty good,
because I have two people that really love me.
You see, things can get better,
and you should know that it was my grandma who made me feel worthless.
People turn out to be so different than who you think they are,
But just know I'm going to be a star.

Disillusionment
by Seylon Edmundson

America, land of the free and the home of the brave.
A place to grow and be your best. It's what many would crave.
Plentiful jobs, many are nice. People are treated fair.
Is it an illusion? A quest? A trick, a trap, a snare?
Misplaced rage, distrust, anger, fear, hate, bias, need for change
Wanting better, but there's unrest. It appears beyond range.
Seeing yourself, mind, body, and soul at a different glance.
It's like a bird leaving a nest, it's fighting, take a chance.
The land of opportunity. It is a work of art.
Many believe it's filled with zest. A gift close to our heart.
Do not be fooled. This is a trick. The land whispers to you.
It is putting you to the test, but this is nothing new.
This is far from fairy tale land, not all dreams will come true.
You will be treated like a pest, only for being you.
With every breath of your being, fight, don't ever repent.
Don't be afraid of the conquest, rid of disillusionment.

Cease To Speak
by Bryce Winn

Silence is at times one's loudest voice
Within their hearts they make a choice
To interfere or cease to speak
To rise above or fall beneath
Obstacles they must overcome
Temptations they will not succumb
If only they will give their best
They will rise above all the rest

Eccentricity
by Jordan Bobbitt

Regrets are pondered by the restless,
While the quiet regret their lack of pursuit.
While pursuit may be the mouse's objective,
The feline's only purpose is utterly irresolute.
Youth find their purpose through passion.
Those of age strive to kindle pleasure amidst their offshoot.
Whereas longevity is bound to an ultimate termination,
Transience is unreachable without eventual destitute.
The restless transform the quiet.
The mouse catechizes the feline.
The youth flourish into the aged.
Longevity meets face to face with transience.

Opposite of White
by Jonathan Williams

I am the soul concealed by oppression
Beat and chained by societal mischief
'Tis my blood which soaks the streets of a nation
I stare only down when life hangs from a cliff
Freedom is mine only desire
Aggression is my whole attire
Pain and misery surrounds my home
As I face the cold grasp of society's moan
I am a king in my own right
Sought to be a peasant
Royalty took from me
Oh how I pray to the heavens
For this I bring the big fight
With those who follow me
I am the opposite of white
And at night everything is me

Light
by Kelsey Bard

in the midst of darkness, light can always be found-
whether it's the moon in the night,
the sun after a raging storm,
or a girl who knows exactly what she wants in the world.

How To Become Successful
by Tovonna Bounds

It's very easy to say what you want,
It's very easy to say what to do.
At the end of the day your dreams are up to you.
Dreams are like goals, goals are achievable,
and when you achieve your goals your reaction is like,
"Whoa unbelievable!" Make your dreams a reality by setting a foundation
and at the end of the rainbow look back at your creation.
All things are possible if you really want it.
You can have anything if you have to have it.
Don't let anyone get in your way, if so tell them to, "Stand away."
Just remember to never give up.
Keep it going because times will get tough.

Shoot To Kill
by Carly McNeill

I pull back my bowstring
and steady my hand.
My prey bows her graceful head
into the wildflower blanket.
Here I wait, silent and still.
The breeze rustles the leaves
and the shade cools my sweating hands.
Sunshine covers the beast,
till her coat glitters like gold.
Here I am ready, silent and still.
Finally, the beast lifts her graceful head.
She turns to look at me, asking why.
I release my arrow and watch it fly.
My prey is hit, right on mark.
The gentle beast turns silent and still.
My kill still has a questioning look.
Asking why I killed the graceful horse
who bears a silver-white horn
and a glittering coat made of gold.
There lies the creature, silent and still.

Never Shall I Forget
by Bridgette Welch

Never shall I forget that day,
that day I was put into question,
which turned my life inside out,
but all I had to do was answer.
Never shall I forget the fear,
the fear that spread throughout my body.
The day I was brought to tears,
was the day I found my true anxiety.
Never shall I forget what I did,
the text message that sent through,
I have ruined myself, my dreams, and life
all because of you.
Never shall I forget that person,
so heartless and so cold.
You turned me in for something so little
and reverted my heart back to stone.
Never shall I forget that day,
that day I was put into question ...

Bruises
by Lauren Sapp

They were fighting. An officer immediately intervened.
It was over when the officer decided to teach him a lesson.
Fists and punches were flying
I didn't understand. I will never understand.
I asked my mom why did he hit the darker colored man
while the man with the lighter complexion just stood there egging him on, jeering.
My mom hurried me along hoping I'd forget, but I didn't.
I never will.
After that I became more aware, I noticed everything.
How my friends with darker skin would flinch every time a police car passed
despite their innocence.
How they would get dirty looks and glares but I would be barely glanced over.
I don't understand why people are colorblind.
I won't understand why they would beat on a seemingly innocent man
That man who probably has a job, a home, a family.
I refuse to understand why he's sent home coated in black and blue bruises
While the other guy gets off with a warning.
We're all the same. We all breathe the same air. We all live in this world.
We all cry. We all bleed.
Which is why it's important for me to understand that hitting another human being
because they are a different skin tone is okay?
But it's not okay. It will never be.

My Heart and My Brain
by Kamia Caldwell

My heart, an organ made for pumping blood.
My brain, the organ that tells everything what it does.
My heart and brain don't work the same.
They don't feel the same pain.
My brain, sees love as a game,
While my heart is left with nothing to do but ache and complain.
My brain, closes out my emotions.
Leaving me to be naive and manipulating at the same time,
Wasting everyone's time but most importantly mine.
My heart wants me to be spontaneously in love,
While my brain makes sure I keep boys at distance and let them wait.
So when push comes to shove I won't feel an ounce of pain.
My emotions and mind will never intertwine and understand each other
enough to make me fine.
My brain and my heart. They are tearing my mind apart!
My heart and my brain. They are driving me insane!
These organs, these hormones, these changes, these crushes, these feelings,
these tears, and this pain.
My brain doesn't want me to get hurt.
So it makes sure my heart doesn't work.

Therapy Session
by Ashley Blackburn

She sits across from me
Drink in one hand and her heart in the other
She has always come to me for therapy
Tears rushing down her cheeks
Clothes disheveled, face as red as a tomato
Fresh bruises that tell of her most recent battle
As she sits across from me she spills- it's about her tyrant husband
I sit there unfazed
He being the topic of each and every one of our sessions
has made me have no sympathy
As she sits across from me, she tells me of his brutal attack
While looking into her face a question erupts from my mind
"Ma'am, why do you stay?"
After I say that she stares into her glass of liquor deeply
All tears cease movement except for one
With all seriousness she looks up at me and says,
"Because he is the only person who will love me."
Then that one tear turns into two
Finally, into a river filled with emotions of sadness,
depression, low self-esteem, hopelessness

The Crow
by Isabelle Husted

Up high sat a crow
On a branch that had died long ago.
It sat above the rotting corpse,
Awaiting for nature to take its course.
The smell was rancid and rank,
It would make your stomach turn to be frank.
But the crow sat above in hunger,
Not thinking of who this was when they were younger.
The rotting corpse of a young girl,
Whose life was great until it began to unfurl.
The crow peered into the lifeless eyes,
The blue covered over with flies.
The crow flew back up to his humble branch,
But his tears poured out like an avalanche.
Who was this girl and what had she done
To deserve a fate ending with no sun.
Her world went dark so quick and fast,
There was no remembering her past.
Up high sat a crow
On a branch that died long ago.

Never Fear a Blank Page
by Maegan Stephens

My plan was to tell you things of happy and sad
Of confusion and wonder
Of a time where I lost myself and was found again.
I could tell you of my love story,
But it's still in the making.
I could tell you of my experiences and my beliefs,
But I wouldn't dare try to influence the path you wish to travel.
Maybe I could even share my words of wisdom,
But I'm afraid I have none, for my knowledge grows from all of the above.
My mind is blank and I hate to have you go on
without gaining something from this silly poem.
After all, isn't that what poetry is for?
Poetry is for embracing your heart within the strokes of a pen
For giving life to the ideas your mind creates.
It makes life so much more beautiful when you're able to take your own beauty
And put it into words that you can pass on to others so they may do the same.
I went into this believing that I had to relay some sort of message to you
One that may possibly change the world or maybe put a smile on your delicate face
But I have come to realize something much bigger than that;
Life mimics the beauty and charisma poetry has because you see,
There is no plan in poetry.

Ride of Our Lives
by Hailey McCool

It's time to ride
We live and die.
But today is the day we celebrate life ...
Wind blowing through our hair
The sound of hooves flying through the air
We pray today to give love and praise.
For this is a love like no other ...
This is the love between a girl and her horse.
And as they close their eyes tonight
They thank Him for the ride of their lives.
For if tomorrow never comes
and the sun doesn't shine
They can at least die happy
Yes, we can die celebrating our lives.
So as I celebrate my life today
Galloping down the paths we made,
I only have one thing left to say:
Thank you, Lord, from both my horse and me,
Oh, thank you, for giving us the ride of our lives!

Are, Not Will
by Alexis Johnson

There is more to us than our figures and flaws,
We have hearts made of silver and gold,
Our worth goes far beyond the scale's numbers,
And the wide range of emotions that may unfold.
We are more than the tardies on our report cards,
And the red 'F's stamped on any test,
We must learn that life is too short to be labeled,
And too short to keep everyone else impressed.
There are days when we seem to forget this,
When the pressure of success is too strong,
Resulting in postponing the ones that we love,
When in the moment is where we belong.
Oh, how much more enjoyable our lives would be,
If we chose to live in the present,
Instead of preparing for the unseeable future,
Leaving the ones that we love discontent.
But if we get the chance to take time and remember,
Instead of counting down the days to any date,
Let's try to enjoy our lives as we know it,
Before time flees and becomes too late.

Sophisticated Chef
by Jennifer Rice

Culinary aromas spilling through the kitchen doors.
Followed by mixing, sifting, and various plates of galore.
She arches over a pot brewing a mixture, yet to be explored.
Numerous people wait to taste the smell
Every serving casts a sweet spell
As you may have guessed, yes, she is a sophisticated chef
Working till every guest has left
Scenes, smells, and sounds have become her second skin
Spices are her accessories, with a slight spin
Cooking is defined as an art
Her soup is like poetry and is the most important part
A chef that frantically creates beautiful appetizers
With no stains on her clean crisp attire
Dancing in timed rhythm around the kitchen, steam rising from sautéed dishes
No need for picky critics to inspect her masterpiece
Each task causes her confidence to increase
She has developed a connection to the ingredients and the utensils
And does not follow the recipes written in pencil
Her various actions are executed in an elegant finesse
A sophisticated chef at its finest

The Beginning
by Lexi Kinkaid

There comes time in every being's life
where they have something that must be done
It tugs and tugs at their hearts until it's done
or the being tries to silence it and go into their everyday life
But then there are the beings who follow that tugging and go with it
I'm only a teenager but my heart started to pull and tug
It wouldn't quit
It was telling my brain something
Every time I write it feels right
So this is for you
This is for myself
This is for the lost one
And for the ones who helped me get me to where I am today
This is my life
My tears
My blood
Myself
The suffering
The falling apart
The love
And finally, the coming back into one as me

Someone
by Annika Robbins

Your friends are there for you every step of the way.
Sometimes when you fall behind they are there to lift you up,
they will help you get away,
They are there even after you are grown up.
Friends help you through hard times,
they come along beside you and encourage you,
even through some of life's hardest climbs,
you will no longer feel blue.
Sometimes you don't think you need help but you really do,
your friends notice things that you won't always see,
so when they come to you, listen too,
they are some of the most caring people to ever be.
They love you with all of your flaws,
and they do not ever judge what you have done,
but are always there to give you applause,
to you they will always be someone.

Sequestered From Reality
by Francesca Horner

Silence is my executioner,
for it can bring about my demise faster than the second hand rounds a clock.
There is no distraction to replace my reality,
therefore I am trapped, grounded inside the four white walls that make up my cell.
I am shackled, incapable of running, unable to escape.
My mind holds me hostage.
My body a ticking time bomb just waiting to explode.
It is as if the past had taken a piece of scorching iron,
and branded my brain with its contents,
so I may never forget the impact it had–
My jail is opened and I, ushered to a stance.
My mind stays stranded in the darkness of the past,
a place I thought I had escaped, only to later discover
that escape was unattainable.
The past holds the rope leash around my neck,
and my floor, finally gave out.
The force of gravity now taking control,
as my body gasps for any available air.
Then, my lifeless body swings in the sharp breeze, like a trophy,
advising the world to avoid a past comparable to mine.

The Sun Will Vanish
by Ally Ramsey

The sun will vanish at the end of day.
Never to return, leaving us in dark.
The flowers and fields will willow away.
Life will be nothing but a finger mark.
Just a matter of time a few days ago.
I saw our beautiful world, it was fine.
We hold our past when we should let it go.
Without a world and a nasty dollar sign.
Crime and murder sweep away the human race.
Leaving nothing but pain and suffering.
We could have avoided in the first place.
By helping the world with recovering.
This world is our home, life, and our one love.
We can't trash it like it's a used up glove.

Here I Am
by Camille Ealey

Do you want to know my secret ... are you sure?
It's nothing significant, it may not even make a difference
But if you're sure ... here I go.
My secret is ... being an open individual
I told you it isn't that significant
It's not important ...
At least I don't think so.
but ... here I am
Just a girl, trying to make it in life.
I'm learning to love myself
So ... here I am.

Golden Asters
by Rebecca Coffey

Glasses of gold, or so I'm told, have such sights for you to see
Such as a peaceful wave of a delicate wildflower ocean
which greets you with a sweet fragile kiss of their soft petals on your lips
While you hold Mother Nature's delicate child to your warm skin
the tart scent seems to melt into the air with the rising dewdrops
which mirror the delicacy of the human eye, caressing the wonder
of how a world could hold such amounts of intense beauty and poise
The treasure of immaculate precision and life that lives deep inside
the vibrant fibers of such a flower, hardly a scratch on the easily broken flesh
is a marvel that with pleasure I gaze upon as I adjust my golden specs.

The Comforter
by Shekinah Brown

Let me be your comforter and hold you tight
Take all your worries away and give you something right
Let me wipe your tears from your face
Kiss you goodnight and hold you tight
I'll hold you till your heart can trust
I'll never leave you or forsake you
I'll stay right by your side and wrap you in my love
I won't tell you lies
I'm the comforter
I'm love in all the right places and times
I'm love that steers your life
I'm Cupid that hit you
I'm what your heart's been waiting for
Who you have been dreaming about at night
I'm your comforter
Won't you let me be your comforter
I'll never let you go and hold you close and tight
Mend your broken heart and make your life all right
I'm the True Comforter, the Holy Spirit

Ode To Butter
by Gracie King

You trickle down the sides of my Walmart brand bread rolls,
and the burnt edges of toast disappear.
You fill up the waffle's sturdy square bread holes,
But I only wish you could be here.
Because my grandma, you see, she has such poor tastebuds
That the fake from the real she can't tell.
She sogged my morning toast with almost real butter suds,
So I had to spit as I wished her farewell.
I sleep with the butter knife, so nobody comes between us,
I'll protect you from my sister and mom.
But I'll make sure they get some, so they will never leave us.
And find more on www.yourbutter.com.
I carry you in my bag when I go to the store,
Just because it's not safe for you to be home alone.
I even gave you a spare key to the door,
And a scribbled out number for the home phone.
And the people, I guess they think I'm insane,
Because my teeth are bright yellow and I stutter,
But they'll never doubt again my soggy, mush brain
When I let them have a taste, oh butter.

It Is
by Madeline Gurganus

Death is glass falling, shattering, breaking
It's nails embedded in a dark coffin
It's a cold shroud of darkness that covers
It's a deafening silence and crushing weight
It's barren fields and sunless daytime skies
Death is a winter that lasts forever
But the living can reside in that winter, too

A Part of Me
by Brooke Moore

There were oceans of fire in her soul,
and her eyes changed colors like the sunsets.
She was a mystery,
But also an open book,
That no one ever read correctly,
Not even herself.
She had darkness but the best kind,
She had gasoline in her veins,
And a wildfire for a mind.
She lived for words but never spoke them,
She has secrets and always wrote them.
She was infuriated and complicated,
but that never stopped her blaze.

Clouds
by Joy Park

What's fluffy and white and floats up high,
Like a pile of cotton in the sky?
And when the wind blows hard and strong,
What very gently floats along?
What shadows above land on a bright day?
"It's just the trees," you might say.
What could get so angry and make a blast?
And then the next moment it has passed.
What brings the rain, what brings the snow?
What showers down on us below?
When you look up high in the sky,
What is that thing you see float by?
White or gray, feathers or cotton balls,
Rain, hail, sleet, or snow from them falls.
Like people, no two are ever the same.
"God, the creator of clouds, is great!" I exclaim.

The Audition For a Chance
by Julia Price

Music is starting, dancers are taking their place
At the barre in the brightly lit studio
Hair slicked back into perfect buns
The air smells of hairspray and hair gel
Everything, the sights, smells, sounds,
Everything appears to be normal
But there is something in the air,
That seems to give away that today is anything but normal
For today, students of the ballet school are competing for the chance to be
In one of the most iconic ballet companies in the world
A chance to be among the best in that company: the ABT,
Or, as it's more commonly known, the American Ballet Theater

You're Beautiful
by Julia Gannon

You're beautiful. Not just in the way you look.
You're beautiful in what you are as well. Your words.
I don't just love them because of the delicate way they roll off your tongue,
but how you use them, the combination of letters.
I scramble to say something more than small talk,
just to hear what your brilliant mind chooses to say.
Because your monologue feeds my brain like no books ever could.
Your personality. Easygoing, but when you are stressed,
you search desperately to find solutions before you're too far under.
But you come back better than ever before.
You can calm me down as easy as a child learns to crawl,
but you make me aware that sometimes it's not always me that needs saving,
it's you. You're confident and strong.
Some think it's rude that when you walk in the hallways,
you don't look at anyone, but more straight ahead.
They may convince themselves you feel you're better than everyone else,
like you think you're above them. But they are so wrong.
It's part of your resolution to stop judging people based on the way they look,
and you explained to me the way to get rid of that is to hit the problem
at the root of it: doing it instinctively.
How you thought of this baffling idea is beyond my comprehension.
Your idea to refrain from even the simplest of judgment just gives you
another perk I admire so. Your kindness opens you up to simply making
unlikely friends, or doing a caring gesture for someone that makes their day
and affects them in ways you can't even imagine.
Your beauty is shown to everyone around you.
And though you may not like the word perfect, that is what you are.
And because of that, you're beautiful.

Angels Among
by Emma Blackburn

In all of time I had heard of none like her
Her words never ran dry
She was always intrigued
A listener and a wonder with the liveliest soul
An exuberant personality
It was strange indeed she was never unhappy
"Is anything impossible?" I would ask.
She would laugh and cup my hand
"It can only be a bump in your road, you choose its size,"
Her smile was a reassurance
There was no rock bottom
But "How?"
"The sun falls too, but it rises each morning."
She would smile and I would wake
And the light would fade, but my hope would remain.

The Holy Matrimony To Lady Justice
by Alexandria Starks

Here comes the bride, here comes the bride,
Dressed in a rope of orange-striped white,
Wearing sterling silver shackles that sparkle in the light.
And as their feet consecrate the marble floor,
They're escorted by the father of the shield, gun, and club.
They make it down the aisle,
The witnessing jury gazes and gasps,
The father giveth his bride to be wed to the groom.
Who reaches over to lift the veil,
Yet, the groom stands tall.
Blindfolded is the groom yet she sees,
A scale in hand and sword clutched tight behind her knees,
She is neither shocked nor surprised,
When the verdict is read,
She taketh this bride to be wed.
For justice has been served today,
Nothing less and nothing more,
Lady Justice never lonely is she,
For she has married every man and woman under the law presiding.

Dream Big
by Shaleah Ford

Dream big, accomplish your goals
Live your life the rest is old
Never give up or try to quit
Put your mind to something and accomplish it
The sky is the limit as you have often heard
Remember that saying and don't forget a word
You can accomplish anything you put your mind to
Get ready, get set because your goals are waiting for you

Selfish Sky
by Carrie George

I knew someone who told me how to feel.
Who took the leaves from trees and sent them to the wind.
He scattered breath and dreams, unreal now that they weren't a part of me.
He drew the Earth with clouds and sky, but left no room for me.
And in the garden where I stood he sent a winter early; my new tomb.
Alone, I wandered ghostly through the wood.
I took the wind upon my lips and sang a song to draw the world again.
I gave myself a land so vast where my voice rang,
and dug a plot for corpses, his new grave.
I caught my leaves back from the selfish sky and buried him so, away, I could fly.

Obscure
by Praise Flowers

His green eyes enrapture me.
They are the kind of green that lacerates its way
through the sordid snow,
reminding you of spring's forthcoming.
They stand out like an abrupt statement
against his paper-colored skin.
I daydream of our limbs
tangled up together and marvel at the disparity.
The notion of us being in tandem turns into a furtive inkling
that I staple to the inside of my eyelids.
I am forever petrified that if I hold my glances any longer,
my eyes will divulge my desires.
So, I cling to makeshift lovers half-heartedly.
As for the better parts of me,
they dangle from the frazzled ends
of his olive sweater.

Beautiful Dangerous Flame
by Gail Harding

You are a lighter.
With one snap, you're a flame.
A beautiful, dangerous flame.
I know you don't always enjoy being a lighter.
I don't always enjoy it, either.
You burn me sometimes, when you're ignited.
Probably because I said something to fuel your fire.
Some of your burns hurt more than others.
But, that's okay, my darling; I need that spark in my life.
Although sometimes it seems as if I'm water,
and it feels like we clash too easily
I can assure you, my beautiful dangerous flame,
water and fire couldn't go better together.
Sometimes it might feel as if someone else is in control of your flame,
like someone is just using your fire for their benefit.
But you must promise me to never, ever run out of fuel.
You must keep going, my beautiful dangerous flame.

It's Not You, It's Me
by Alex Brewington

I open my heart to you,
And I am forced to instantly close it again.
Because in a millisecond I have found something that I hate.
Something about you.
Even in the midst of your perfection,
I have reached into the darkest parts of my mind
And found a reason to hate you.
A reason to close my heart again.
You are kind, but maybe too kind.
You are funny, but you do not make me laugh hard enough.
And you care, possibly too much,
About me and the things that I like.
You have wrapped yourself around me
Like a warm blanket that is meant to protect me from the world.
But what I really need protection from is myself.
My obsessive mind.
My destructive heart.
Maybe I am afraid of the feelings that will come pouring out of me.
Feelings that I have trapped inside my heart.
Like Pandora's box, it is a mystery to even me.

The Grief
by Kasey Word

My parents, my teachers,
and all the books I've read
Could not have prepared me
For the relentless onslaught of tidal waves
That would crash into me over and over
Unceasing until I'm drowning.
It's been months and some days,
I think I've moved on, up, and past it.
But then a song comes on,
I find your red Santa sweats,
Or something happens at school
And I remember that you'll never pick up the phone again.
It's not a chore, a task, or a check off of my to-do list.
It's forgiveness, acceptance, adjustment.
It's learning how to continue loving you
Unconditionally,
Only now,
From a distance.

Pink Lemonade Ladies
by Jayde Huffman

Do you know what they do
While they rearrange their face or die for those red shoes?
Can you hear what they say
As they walk in circles until they have their way?
Oh, but they need this to survive the day.
But do you know who they are?
You can tell by what they kill.
They are foxes with fur coats,
And snakes with hot high heels.
They have one eye, one ear and seven sour mouths.
Careful, better watch what you let out.
Pink lemonade ladies have to stay whole,
Shallow ladies with shallow souls.
Oh, but what better to do
While they make their strands brand new?
Do you know what the ladies
Say about you?

She Smiles As She Weeps
by Jade Edwards

She smiles as she weeps.
If you know this, then you know her.
You know she's made of shards of glass
That vanish in the plastic darkness
And crumble in the earthen light.
You know she'll never play a card
But she'll play the strings,
Play the blame-game,
Play like a vindictive child with her toys.
So she'll lash and she'll bully and she'll break
And she'll leave the cleaning for the mess.
So she'll forget a promise and a favor and even a playmate
Over a doll already lost to indifference.
But feel no anger towards her, for she has long succumbed to her own grief.
If you know this, then you know her.
She smiles as she weeps.

I Am Kevin
by Erika Garcia

Please don't think this is a curse, in fact it could be much worse
Even though I live in my own world, I still hear every word
Yes I may kick and shout, but I am still figuring things out
It isn't anyone's fault I have the disorder, instead I think I'm quite in order
Sometimes I get angry because people look at me and don't understand
However God made me, so take me as I am
Don't think I'm the only one, Mozart, Bill Gates and Einstein have it too
There's one of me in every 42, but there's only one me, and I'm such a joy!
Without me, life would be a bore
My family keeps me warm like a blanket on my back,
and yet they don't complain about what I lack
Yeah I may be hard to deal with, but my family thinks I'm quite dreamy
I don't get mad all the time like you think I do,
actually I have a very happy side too
I may not make many friends,
but I know that I can count on my family like someone holding my hand
Days of no talking are over, and I actually talk way more
I am who I am, so take me as I am or leave me
I'm autistic, and I'm very proud to be me!

Inescapable
by Zachary Homan

Happiness is a disease
You won't understand until you are infected
Happiness is unavoidable
You will be taken before you even realize
Happiness will take over

Society vs. Teens
by Anna Yoo

"High school will be the best four years of your life," she said to the class of 2016.
Seven different alarms to make sure I wake up at six am. The clock hits three a.m.-
it is late because even after 8 full hours of learning nothing about the real world,
such as self-defense, how to finance and live alone ... you still must work at home
and relearn all the pointless things about why Charlie's water turned blue after
he mixed it with a chemical ... High school will be the best four years of your life.
The lectures from "your skirt is too short" to "the boys will be distracted"
even though you just like that coral pink colored skirt
High school will be the best four years of your life.
The pressure from parents about what college you want to attend
and what you want to do with the rest of your life.
Your father making you play soccer because he was great at it
when he was in high school. High school will be the best four years of your life.
The expectations from a older sibling. "Why can't you be more like her?"
Friendships being made and broken because of trust and who has more or less.
The "I love you" and heartaches. High school will be the best four years of your
life. Finally, learning to love yourself and who you are and finding the people
you vibe with. High school is like a slap on the wrist… however it was a pan that
slapped you.. And that pan was on fire and you are stuck to the ground,
you can fall and cry and hide or you can recover and learn. Seems all so simple
to adults but the way we see it is completely different. High school will not be
the best four years of your life. High school is the reality check every child gets.
High school is a place you make mistakes so you can learn from them
and not make them in the real world. Our life depends on how we do as a teenager,
a teen is also a minor, a child and it is so scary.
However, they do not get to decide what is wrong from right.
If you like that skirt wear it because that is what you like.
If you do not want to play that sport then don't because that's what you want.
If you prefer a different college then change it because it's your life and future.
Academics do not and will not define who you are, nor do your actions.
It is how you grow up little by little and learn.
There will always be obstacles you face and that is okay
because you have time to fix them.
High school will not be the best four years of your life.

My Truth
by Julianna Rowan

It is always important to tell the truth,
Whether you are in rain, sunshine, or snow.
Sometimes it hurts the way a truth may go.
With that in mind, I tell you I do not like these four halls;
I cannot stand it here between these concrete walls.
They have provided me with this binding label,
But the truth is that's one great big fable.
Having an inner circle is not very cool.
It's not a fair place at all, this school.
Twelve days from now I will wave goodbye with a smile,
And I will stay gone for a very long while.
You see, y'all will not even miss my face
Because I was never a huge part of this place.
I tell you this, but you won't even listen:
Leaving this place is my own decision–
I do not want to be here anymore.
I hope that does not make you very sore.
Now I have a question for the teacher of this class:
Will you show me forgiveness and allow me to pass?
I told you my honest-to-goodness truth.

Autumn In His Eyes
by Stephanie Wiegmann

Rain of rubies and topazes cascade from the trees,
Protesting blatantly in crunches underneath my feet.
While longing winds tug curiously at my scarf and hair.
Gleefully spreading the word that soon winter shall be here.
Large warm hands engulf my delicate creamy fingers,
While our shuffling feet are quick to linger.
Amber sparks breaking through the cool peridot ponds in his eyes.
If he should steal a kiss in this autumn shower no one would be the wise.
Leaves are bidding their last farewell to their emerald hue.
Reluctantly I take my time to say goodbye to you.
As the new season drapes its golden coat around the trees.
My heart beats rapidly threatening to flee.
How precise the timing I should fall with the leaves.
Beneath my skin trembling, for my love you have thieved.
A gentle peck on the cheek sets my skin blazing.
Oh what splendor it is to go October gazing!
Amber sparks breaking through the cool peridot ponds in his eyes.
Oh how he does make this fall come alive!
Though often the season marks the end of a time.
I am perfectly at peace knowing this autumn won't leave his eyes.

When?
by Trinity Haskins

The year 2016, supposedly a season of hopes and dreams
Remember when you said, "New Year, New Me"?
Back to your old habits, no change, I see.
You said, you'd try new things and view new panes;
be confident and take chances.
Don't doubt yourself. I know you can handle it.
Don't wait, dear, it's time to begin.
If not now, then when?

Adventure
by Minha Asif

I wish for adventure so really bad
I wish for adventure so much, I think I'll go mad!
I'm supposed to be at Hogwarts, riding the magical train
I'm supposed to be quizzing a sphinx, who has the smartest of brains
I'm supposed to be at the Hunger Games, trying to stay alive
I'm supposed to be training for Dauntless while trying to survive
I'm supposed to be a spy trying to find a traitor named Day
I'm supposed to be learning how to use a wand in so many ways
There're so many things that I really want to be
But all of them fade when reality hits me
They may not be real or so as it seems
But one thing's for sure, they'll stay alive in my dreams!

The Fox and the Mouse
by Katie Brooks

Soft, red fur,
Thin, black snout,
From the bush he's under,
Sniffing out a mouse.
Quick, lean creature,
Little brown mouse-
He's struggling to reach her
In her little mouse house.
Short, soft fur,
Quick brown mouse,
Smart little creature
Trembling in her house.
Smart, but can he reach her?
Quick, she leaves her house!
No longer does he see her,
Intelligent little mouse.

Colder Than You
by Trinity Lassiter

I grew cold while you were away
I remember begging you to stay
I knew I'd never be enough for you
Still I tried to be the best for you
Even when you left me broken and bruised and in shatters
I still hear your voice cursing and asking, what does it matter?
I still taste the ghost of our first kiss
But now all I can feel are your fists
I wanted you like nothing else I'd wanted before
I'd been so stupid to think you wanted me more
And even now when I'm covered in black and blue
I swear I will only ever love you
Even when I'm the one you've left brokenhearted
I'm still crying over my dearly departed

ESPROC TREE
by Adriana Benjamin

"Pravus isn't for everyone son. Enter at your own risk."
These words echoed in his brain while he sat still, quiet, unmoving,
underneath the town's center; a tall and majestic hardwood center.
He sat and watched each of God's creatures go about their day,
not a face unturned or bothered by the paralyzing cold and howling wind.
Leaning back onto the trunk, he drifted into an overpowering sleep.
This was when he came to him, a second time. The sagging, wrinkled face and
hollowed eyes of his greeter penetrated his mind, clearing it of any other thoughts;
along with his jet black hair, untouched by dye, not a gray to be found,
sitting on his head like a sea of crows complementing the bleak winter sky.
The frightened traveler's eyes shot open, only to find himself
stationed underneath the tree, his Bible still open in his lap.
Gathering his items to leave, he and a fierce pair of hollowed eyes met.
He stared into the traveler's soul with a look of fiendish greed and satisfaction.
Standing with his back towards the tree, the traveler could not shake the feeling
of a force pulling him back towards the tree.
Turning around, hundreds of pairs of dead eyes appeared within the foliage,
devouring his soul, extending their limbs from every direction
bringing him in closer and closer.
Author's note: Not everything is best understood forwards

I Am From
by Tala Alomary

I am from Metro-Mississippi
Where all the "yeehaws" and the "howdys"
are "good mornings" and "how are yous"
I am from northern Jordan
Where my summers are filled with the dancing heat
And my cousins yelling at me to speak in English
I am from the shin guards and the tutus
From the soccer fields and dance studios where I "try harder and do your best!"
To kick a ball while practicing my croisé derrière
I am from the homemade golf courses in my yard,
The sounds of my mother scolding "stop digging holes near my roses and mints!"
I am from my love of creativity, my poetry and drawings, the paintings and the lyrics
That drive my nights into a sweet blissful
Harmony of words and colors coming together
I am from the mud of the Dead Sea and the water of the Mississippi
My homes away from home

2:04 AM
by Fatimah Williams

When will I be truly happy
As I lay my head down at night
I think about all the wrong things I've done
All the selfish things I've done
All the good things I've done
But why don't my good actions bring me happiness
Is it because the bad outweigh the good
No matter how good, the bad will always outweigh because it is bad
So when will happiness come to me
I feel I've lost the energy to chase it
There are things that make me happy
Am I happy or am I satisfied
How can you tell the difference
If you're not sure what true happiness feels like
How can you tell the difference
If you think you're sure
But how can you be sure that you are sure

Dulcet Discrepancies
by Luke Pleasant

You say that I am perfect,
Despite my imperfections and flaws.
You promise that my beauty is the cause
Of all the ludicrous looks, strained silence, and dropped jaws.
You promise that my heart you will guard and protect.
You say my golden locks can hypnotize,
As they wave gently in the smooth cyan tide,
That there is nothing more captivating the whole world wide.
You make me believe that there is no reason to run and hide.
My insecurities you promise not to criticize.
You say you can get lost forever,
Staring into my livid blue eyes.
Your words are so sweet, they couldn't be lies.
As we lie here under the mango and coral skies,
We feel as if we will just blow away with the zephyr.
You say that in an ocean of passion our minds can swim.
You say that we can nestle together under this palm tree.
You say that together our hearts were meant to be.
You say that you love me,
But you know, that you love him.

Hero In Me
by JerMarcus Black

I spent every second of my life alone
I was nice and generous to everyone
Was I doing anything wrong?
Life full of sadness
But one day, I found a cure to all my madness
I met a new friend named Harry
He was always by my side
Nothing to me was scary
We were together every ride
My mom didn't like him
But I don't care what she thinks
She kicked me out of her house
But I still had Harry to keep me on my feet
Everything was great until me and Harry had a fight
I then told him I need a break
But he wanted me to stay tight, so I took him one more time
After I took him, Harry saw me take my last breath
There he laughed at my death
It's too late to not take Harry again
Harry was heroin

The Beloved
by M. Jensen Lee

Men to the left.
Women to the right.
Eight words, simple words.
See the chimney flames?
You will be burned to cinders and ash.
Don't cry, run Angel of Death.
His machine gun trained on us,
our illusions left behind.
My dreams are now prisoners in barbed wire.
In Auschwitz sunshine is hidden by the smoke of corpses.
Yet you still tell us, "Have faith in life."

My Silence
by Regan Cook

Noise fills the space around me, but not within me;
my silence inside absorbs my thoughts, thoughts of grief and loss.
my silence is my stronghold; it calms me and allows my thoughts to roam free.
my silence isn't darkness as many may see.
I can feel my silence wrapping around me.
lost in my silence, I can no longer hear the noise outside;
I am calm and free.

A Flower Made of Glass
by Julia Sullivan

In your garden I'm a flower made of glass
planted amongst the others in the grass.
To plainly rest statically in the breeze
and gaze at the whole world and not just the trees,
leaves anyone watching frightened and aghast.
My edges are transparent, quite in contrast,
to their petals whose colors will never last.
The tips of my blossom are gawked at with ease
in your garden.
Weeks after loads of their complaining you asked,
"Why do you have to be such a sheer outcast?"
I replied quickly unwilling to appease,
"Me? Your flowers permeate the vain disease!"
Truth of your blemished blossoms came out at last
in your garden.

Dancing Dead Leaves
by Julia Shipman

Vibrant colors brighter than the sun
Fall to the earth and cover the grounds
Like a crisp, dry blanket that crushes beneath my feet
When the winds pick up they dance with great glee
Just for me, they put on a show
Captive by their festive colors
Melancholy is not what I feel when they come a halt
The leaves appear to be dead
And I remember, they are dead
The winds cry for them to dance again
But they have already turned from light to brown
But I know
They'll come again
And they'll fall again
And they'll dance again
For me, they will.

House of Wolves
by Carlos Gort

My skin stalking me, smothering me
Falling into another hole again
The smell of iron blood in the air
I can hear them gnawing at the door
Wolves come out from the floorboards
I tell them to sharpen their teeth
Just when I thought I was safe
The pack engulfs me in hate
Serrations in the skin only grow deeper
Could you see the hell in my eyes?
The fear hanging down from my neck?
The laughter when they tore me to pieces?
Blood drenched flesh mangled in my teeth
Cannibalistic, nihilistic, self-loathing wolf
Lurking in the back of my mind
I await again for my time to strike
Tearing this house down brick by brick
The fire raging into my lungs
I howl at the dead of night waiting for the sun
As I rip myself from limb to vein

Fall!
by Patricia Addis

Fall, it's finally here!
It's time to clap, it's time to cheer!
It's time for pumpkin spice lattés
but sadly, it's the end of swimming all day
It's time for the holiday thrill
but it's the end of pool water chill.
It's almost time for Halloween costumes
and it's finally the end of those horrible chlorine fumes.
It's nearly time to carve pumpkins and set up the scarecrow
and plus there won't be so much grass to mow!
It's just about time to eat bags upon bags of candy
but don't expect your toes to still be sandy.
I can't wait to reunite with family!
Oh no! There won't be anymore chilling under the shady cherry tree.
Fall, it's my favorite time of year,
especially since Christmas is nearly here!

December 10, 1998
by Justin DeShong

December 10, 1998 on this day, a child came to this world
Just a regular, not one used for heir of riches or for the underworld
That day God, the Almighty King, said, "Let there be this child,
A child that will have 3 brothers, under a family that is not wild."
This child, this child, he came to this world on a Thursday,
And this child, this child had yellow as the color of favoritism and not gray
Yes, this child chose to be a Christian and follow his personal savior
And always, with his personal savior will always succeed and have no failure
December 10, 1998 on this day, a child came to this world
And was taken care of, never was damaged or curled
That day a mother, released many moments of stress and pain
And she released a discipline child, not one that needed a chain
This child, this child, he came to this world with patience
Waiting for the return of his personal savior, his acquaintance
Always, he will obey and listen to his personal savior
December 10, 1998 on this day, a child came to this world
With a will that was to go with his personal savior to the dream world
That day a father, was happy to see his second-born son
And he followed him to the other stages of after-birth watching the son he won
This child, this child, he came to this world at the right time
For he is self-disciplined, not used for evil or to commit a crime
Always, this child will be remembered by the ones he is loved by

Arena
by Thaiyir Sanders

The pen is mightier than the sword
When black ink spills, I holler for more
The crowd can be cheering and screaming
But I'd be all too absorbed, rewriting and proofreading
I make my point with periods
I mark my words in cursive
I take the hardest lessons from my life, write them down and make them worth it
I block with commas, then continue the attack
I do not need a run-on sentence to push all of my enemies back
I indent paragraphs, but never break the flow
I capitalize on my opportunities on the word, "Go!"
I'm a gladiator
Armed with pen and paper
And the ink I'm covered in
Is all that I savor
Do you dare enter my coliseum and do battle in the Writer's Arena?

The Purging Flame
by Steven Blalock

I woke at noon on a dreary day
The sun hid behind the clouds from the inferior life below
The clouds threatened to swell then empty their bellies onto the mountains
The afternoon of that day was dry as old bones
The sun had come out to greet his subjects below
He shone his heated rays down onto the mountains
But it was too much for the trees
One little spark of friction was all it took
For the trees to erupt and succumb to the burn
I looked from my empty watchtower and beheld the sight
The flame burned away the impurity of the land
No animals could be seen. They must have all gone
The purging flame grew brighter and crawled along
It was a beautiful sight in its own way
Amazing it was that such destruction was making way for life
Flowers would sprout and bloom in slow grace
It would give a view of beauty to those who look below
And it will give color to the vulcanized mountains
I had woken at noon on a lovely day

Maybe
by Jaden Buchanan

Maybe one day I'll be this fearless girl, who's not afraid to show the world
To conquer all her fears and accept no defeat
Maybe one day all my problems will go away
Vanishing like the tears in the rain with no trace
Maybe one day I could fix my mistakes
Go back in time so there won't be no more guilt and hate
Maybe one day my life will be so much easier
Not having to having to carry so much weight at one time would be like a breather
Maybe one day I will try even harder
To push myself to the best and go even farther
Maybe one day I could make everybody happy
Not disappoint them to the point where I know I'm not worthy
Maybe one day I can feel what love is
Love is like war, but at the end I'll still be his
Maybe one day everything will be okay
No fighting, no arguing, just peace without any pay
Maybe one day I will be free from all the pain
Break from all the chains that's keeping me away
Maybe today I will push all those thoughts away
And believe in myself just maybe one day

Perfection?
by Sumaiyah Taliah Kee

Smiles and laughs, is that all you see?
I don't like to share but I guess it's time you know about me.
On the outside I am completely fine.
Yes. You wouldn't expect the pain I hide.
It's easy to cover up because no one suspects.
But most times I'm a huge mess.
The pressure of perfection haunts me.
The strain to intangible feelings taunt me.
I AM HUMAN.
But what does that mean?
Robot they should have called me.
All I know is getting it right and not giving up until I've given a fight.
But then what's next?
Vexed with pain.
There's nothing else I can gain but that stupid look of shame.
Some seem to win at this game called life.
But at times I wonder will I have enough energy to fight.
Will there be anything left?
After I've reached all my success.
Will there be someone to tell me I did it.
Or will they tell me I didn't have enough to "Fit It"

Sheep In Wolf's Clothing
by Christopher Merlos

Though we are all leaves
stemming from the same branch
attached to the same trunk
Though we all are grounded by
the same deep roots
We couldn't be more divided.
Those of high power spit poison on the weak
Paying my people slave wages
while proclaiming us criminals
They expect our servitude
Then wage war using our soldiers
They proclaim the blood and bones
and flesh of my family members illegal
Hard workers searching for the American Dream
only to find a Star-Spangled Nightmare
We come courageously to the Land of the Brave
only to be met with boots crushing our necks
and chains wrapped around our wrists
We are not who they say we are
We are sheep in wolf's clothing

Unity
by India Street

We are a nation united
We are a nation of the free
So we must not be divided
And be the best we can be
We must all work together
Know what's right and wrong
Not choose the easier path
Just because it's not as long
'We' is the start of our constitution
Not I or just you
So won't you be the resolution
And take a look at another's point of view
No life is worth more than the next
No color above them all
No race should be shamed upon
Or our ignorance will be our downfall
Treat everyone with kindness
Your weapon the power of love
Equality must be for everyone
For us to rise above

A Poem of Self-Empowerment
by Hope Burke

Avoid people who make you rethink every decision you've made.
Avoid people who make you anxious.
Avoid people who make your stomach twist into knots.
Avoid people who belittle you and question your worth,
because you are beautiful.
Acknowledge your strengths, and don't let anyone tell you you aren't enough.
Brush them off because you are a masterpiece and all art has critics.

Ode To Nutella
by Tanner Fant

Nutella, oh Nutella, how do I love thee?
Let me count the ways.
Oh how its great, rich taste fills me
While on my bed I lay
Brown and creamy is its look
Better than thy richest chocolate thee hath ever seen
One more bite and thou wilt be hooked
If thee look hence I wilt licketh it clean
Thou touch my Nutella I wilt be mad
Be smart, stay away, and let me eat
Get thy own jug and thou wilt be glad
Thou disobey my rules thou wilt be beat
Oh Nutella, thou knoweth how to make my day
Although later my hips will sadly pay

Fall: the Perfect Time
by Taylor Degges

Time for hoodies and lattes
Time to say goodbye to summer weather
And hello to fall weather
From Halloween to Thanksgiving
What a wonderful time of laughter and joy
As it gets us ready for the next season
From pumpkin patch to turkey pot pie
It's the mix of summer and winter
Not too hot and not too cold
It's the perfect time
To have some fun
When fall leaves
It's time to wait for next year
To have the same fun again

Smile
by Taylor Deadwyler

Face polished, teeth whitened, face anew
Tags still thread in cloth, sun glaring at your skin
Nerves shot, head low, you walk in
Walk in to your future, walk in to judgmental stares
Oh how those stares never change
Fear creeps in, silence stays, can't they just look away
I wish I could leave like the wind
Blend in so pain won't find me
Is there something that I did, for I don't know any evil
That I would condemn this torment to
Can it just be over
When will I learn that darkness has consumed
It whistles as it consumes, smiles as light is taken
Why can I only see the darkness, it hides behind fake joy
Joy that used to be real till the greed in this world destroyed it
All evilness was good once
Then this cruel world corrupted the good
With its shiny cars and brand name clothes
I walk with that very real fake joy every day
Waiting for the day I forget that it's fake
Like so many others have forgotten before me, smile

My Plea
by Wy'Kia Frelot

As I felt my brain deteriorate,
A glass wall was built
One where I could see, but never join the true world
And I'd see the smiles
But never connect
And I'd see the love,
But always doubted it
In the dark, I would ponder
What would happen if I wandered
Far away from those who claimed to love me
Would they cry?
Would they get on with their lives?
I always imagined when it happened
That I'd sit from the distance that I always thought was real
And I'd see them mourn,
But then they'd get over it
And I seem to scream my feelings out loud
But no one has ever heard my cries
Please, don't let anyone end up like me

Guantanamo Bay
by Regan Harrison

A little island girl,
Clothed in a stained t-shirt and ripped gym shorts
Climbing trees and listening to the silent steps of the stagnant iguana.
Eyes filled with wonder and excitement for adventure that lies ahead.
A little island girl,
Unaware of the dangers that are taking place.
Unaware of the ninety-one terrorists in her front yard.
Unaware of the deceitful dictator in her backyard.
A little island girl,
Gracefully galloping along the seashore.
Blind to the negative media propaganda,
Blind to the danger the men and women in uniform encountered,
Blind to the historical importance.
A little island girl,
Now fully grown and moved away,
Facing new excitement and adventure.
Now fully aware of the dangers.
Now fully willing and able to face the dangers of wearing that uniform.

Balsam Sounds
by Alexander Kirov

Up high, one finds primeval forests in Eyrolours
Yet once stepped down, visible sky extends into the clouds
Bringing duller trails of blackened flowers to the waiting,
Hidden with balsam sounds. Silent trees to unconditioned
Ears are covered in snow, clearly there is nothing to hear.
It is of the smell we think when strolling with balsam firs.
But to those who steer low in the clouds, gray as richest fur,
Of thicker nights, of sicker plights can hear the beating sounds.
"I fear today is nowhere near the profit we hold dear
And when she asks why the men are unfathomably seared,
I gently say that because we sleep, others toil still."
Not enough, the sky should be blacker.
Higher in Eyrolours, with mountains of cragged ridges,
Of standing brickstone bridges where soiled water niches
As if stormed, torrential. Not enough, the sky was grayer.
But with each such passed storm, the water is only lower,
Every move, the content only higher. Unbearable
Heat, high within Eyrolours, the balsams cry to Her
With inhuman clairvoyance and expect the Terrible,
And the birds sing no more. Not enough, we were once greener.

Premier Amour
by Arden Spearman

Thrum of beryl
Weld steadfast
Wound about my nape
It has always last
The gem, eternally steady
Only changed by the mark of love
Lilac emerges for a new age
Prognosticated from gods above
A vicennial has transpired
Plethoric visages seemed ubiquitous
Till a scintillation of hue egressed
Lilac emanated litigious
I watched for a glimpse of my divination
A figure arose within the violet stone
My aperture perceived indubitably
For the form was my own

Luminescence
by Joshua Goeltz

Once the light has been revealed to you
it is inescapable
you open your eyes and there it is
filing into you.
But you still blink,
and you look away,
you even close your eyes,
but the image will stay.
You may decide that you want
to hide from what asks
only that you see it
and allow it to guide you.
Never despair, for even the blind
will know the light
by the description of another,
and regardless of whether you even decide
to allow the light inside
it will always touch you,
and you will always know it is there

46,001
by Lauren LeDonne

Bang Bang ... trembling hands ... one
A deep monotone voice spits statistics through speakers
People fall to bodies—bodies create numbers
-- beats engulf my mind
I forget, because that would never happen to me
Bang Bang ... paralyzed eyes ... five
A cold dismal voice rattles off names through the fluorescent screen
Relatives mourn beloved names—names create lists
-- clicks change the channel
I forget, because that would never happen to me
Bang Bang ... shivering hands ... twenty
A dull sorrowful voice echoes out to the crowd
Families sob—sobs pour into the ears of loved ones
-- we drive by
I forget, because that would never happen to me
Bang Bang ... cold body ... forty-six thousand
This time, I did not listen to the radio, watch the news, or look away
This time, the next song never played,
the channel never changed, the car never drove past
Because it did happen to me
Forty-six thousand and one

Our Love Will Continue On
by Alexis Antola

Heath I loved; he captured my heart
The bond of love a gift.
He received a call, felt a duty to honor;
To defend our country made my heart grow fonder,
We soon married with one week of bliss;
Receiving his orders, off he went.
To fight a war, knowing not what was in store
His only words: letters.
Now nine months apart
I receive less than from the start
Reading of chaos and death, I hold my breath ...
Two weeks now- no word;
My worst worry afeard.
In the middle of the night,
I dream my love tells me, "It will be all right."
Months have passed- a knock on the door,
Two officers, handing me dog tags call him a "hero,"
I lost my love, but not forever,
That short time together
We conceived a daughter: Heather.

My Life
by Justin Williams

If in my guess to achieve my goals
I stumble or crumble and lose my soul
Those that knew me would easily co-sign
There was never a life as hard as mine
No father, no chance, and no guide
I only follow my voice inside
If it guides me wrong and I do not win
I'll learn from mistakes and try to achieve again

Bottomless
by JaQuaria White

I don't really mean anything to anybody
As time passes, I slowly close myself emotionally
My heart is at a standstill, not knowing which direction to travel
I don't really mean anything to anybody
I watch every minute go by.
Still no message.
The one who claims to love me, won't pick up what keeps us in communion.
I don't really mean anything to anybody
When I'm left alone, dark clouds attempt to ruin the sunny thoughts in me.
Don't want to question; everything is always no
In due time, special things are going to change
Tears will fall, feelings will diminish, happiness will fade, love will disappear
I don't really mean anything to anybody

Driving (Peace)
by Julia McCall

Just driving down the road,
It is something we don't do very often,
but when we do it is amazing.
Watching the road go by,
Knowing I don't have to worry about anything, but the passing world.
As soon as we stop, and the music turns off,
And there is no more talking,
But silence for those few seconds,
I realize my favorite time is in the car.
Who would have thought driving in the car could be so peaceful.
"Good-bye Old Blue," you say, so the car knows you are thankful
And then life goes on.

The Playground
by Nicole Horstemeyer

My mind is a playground
On a bright summer's day.
Many thoughts run around,
Feelings tease and play.
My emotions run quick
In a big game of tag,
Never sure which one's "it"
And beginning to lag.
After tag, hide-and-seek!
Moticarions' the star,
Invisible when needed;
I look near and look far.
Certainty rides the see-saw,
Sink down and wink up.
If decisions should come,
I can't make my mind up!
Peace comes in the night
With sleep as its host.
The playground is vacant
Except for my ghost.

Lily Flower
by Zoey Hicks

The hues of her existence are vibrant and enticing,
she simply touched me and I sprang to back to life,
love pours from her dainty palms,
beauty of countless rising moons seeps from her veins,
she is my lovely lily flower,
blossoming into a dazzling dance of colors,
swimming, moving, weaving in and around my vision,
she spoke to me and transformed me,
she's overflowing with joy and grace,
I looked upon her and fell in love,
I love her in a way I cannot comprehend,
she is magnificent,
those eyes like diamonds, that smile like a streaking star,
she is like a worn, yet cherished old book, handsomely packaged,
yet under appreciated by those who've not the time to read her,
she is all I never knew I wanted,
yet she is like the graceful doe, like the passing rain shower, like the roaring flame,
she is fleeting, never around for too long,
so all I'm left to do is smile, even though my insides twist and tear,
as if in losing her,
I will lose myself as well.

Photo
by Ryan Smearman

Mom and Dad lying
In a hospital bed
A sweet newborn baby
Hoping to be fed
Sitting and waiting
Under the covers
His little feet show
And begin to shudder
And without a doubt
I wish I was present
To share in that juncture
To share in the portent
For now I will look
At all of the pictures
That you were so lucky
To get to share with her
For now just be happy
Just live long and prosper
Because all has to end
And you need something to offer

Can·cer/noun/A Reminder
by Hannah Marston

From walking, to walker, to wheelchair,
from gold locks, to bald spots, to completely receded hair.
They think I'm breathing fine, but I'm drowning in the pain,
the poison is igniting, scorching in my veins,
an innocent life, exceptionally strained,
I am a trapped prisoner in the chemo's chains.
Here I ponder, recalling life before the hazardous rays:
times full of passing time, now anxiously counting down my days.
This still feels surreal; I cannot heal this fear,
struggling bones, sunken face, my end for sure is near.
See the gratefulness in this wretched mess,
a gain of wisdom and a feeling of content,
a horrendous disease known to tear families apart,
serves as a reminder to cherish every moment.
Regard the life of living in dread,
the precious moments so dear slip fast,
bond with family and live your life's passion,
you never know when the day is your last.

Nobody Is a Nobody
by Hannah Cooper

Everybody is somebody
and no one is alone ...
Although some feel like nobody
we all have at least one
who remains faithful.
A bosom friend-
loves 'til the end
and never leaves remorseful.

The World In Vivid Color
by Gabriella Merced

The world is vivid in color
From season to season it changes in Technicolor
Summer lives in vibrant greens and jubilant blues
Then to the next hues
Fall breathes in burnt umber and crisp yellow
Then the next colors follow
Winter sparkles in melancholy blue and diamond white
The next colors sneak in like dawn's sunlight
Spring grows in petal pink and pastel blue
Then the world shifts back into summer's hue

Poke a Plant
by Ansley Davies

You mustn't poke a plant
I ask my grandma why it is I can't
Because precious plants must be protected
So they don't feel dejected.
For bushes, brambles, and even a bitty brier
Too tired
Of being pushed and prodded.
As she spoke I nodded
But I had to ask if it is really true
That plants feel like me and you
Just because they don't speak
That doesn't mean that they don't become weak.
So I pitied the poor, precious plant
And decided that I just can't poke a plant.

Eye of the Beholder
by Essence Epperson

You spent all your time,
Trying to catch someone's eye,
While the rest of your life passes you by,
All for a girl who didn't know your name,
And for a boy who was only interested in playing games,
You call her your babe,
While someone else calls her "mine,"
You think she's into you?
You're wasting your time,
People with closed minds and open eyes,
Follow those who are "beautiful,"
But beauty is a disease afflicted onto human beings,
Beauty hides true feelings and personality,
You were focused on the clothes he wears,
And the shoes he buys to impress,
But he was really a monster in dress,
But you would never know until you've invested your time in someone
you were only interested in because of how they look.

For Old Times' Sake
by Annabelle Milne

Who would have thought the ice cold glass dripping with condensation
could make you feel so warm and cozy,
like drinking steamy hot chocolate on a frosty winter's night.
Your body shivering and craving warmth can only stand so much
of the seasonal change. The sweltering hot chocolate is tempting you
and reading your trembling ice blue lips, inviting you to take a swig or two,
asking that you temporarily forget about your responsibilities
and indulge just like old times. Knowing your past you better not
but it's been a long, overwhelming winter, your body is bitter and weary,
it's just so exhausting doing the right thing all the time.
After contemplating what seems like forever your sober mind surrenders
listening to the devil on your shoulder. "Oh what the heck," as your mouth fills
with liquid gold sent from the gods, instantly feeling repaired and young again,
youth is revived yet so dehydrated, you bleed for another taste, another love.
Quick, come up with a new excuse, a new face to blame
so you can drown yourself in yet another familiar mug of hot chocolate.
But what your old drunk self could never seem to remember
was that the hot chocolate didn't stay hot forever,
and this was just the very start of a prolonged, unpredictable winter.

The Secret Mission
by Faisal Mohammed

I softly totter to the target
Hoping to secure a source of sustenance
Pupils dilate, reducing the obscurity
My shadow sneaking beside me.
The rasping of the floorboards
Attempting to reveal my location
My mission: to cease my appetite
With an amusing wedge of a velvety pastry,
The aroma tingling my nose, alerting me of my advancement.
But forever foiled, by the barking of futile creature
Loyal?
Only to the enemy. Mom and Dad.

The Remains of My Imagination
by Patricia Harvel

Lost and alone.
My life is a rose.
Except for the stem,
A fire is ignited at one end.
The rose flourishes in a garden on my heart.
My mind is the gasoline,
The petals are my dreams.
My fire sits just above my throat.
Every bad decision makes my fire grow.
Kindness is the key to put my fire out.
Except there is a problem,
The world is never fair,
And kindness is rare.
So now my stem is bare.
My rose petals are no longer there.
My fire has reached my heart.
There is no more air.
The life cycle of my divine garden was not long.
The worst part is that I think my soul is forever gone.

Dream Chaser
by Mariyana Woods

When you have a feeling inside: determination, dedication, a feeling of greatness.
You're telling yourself you want to make it, but you have no motivation.
Negativity surrounding you, telling you the opposite of your feelings lately.
"She's not good enough," but you fake a smile
because you know the noise in the background is only hating.
Praying, waiting for your downfall.
Your friends will be the ones to wish you well, but have you looking lost.
Don't trust them, don't trust them.
They'll kill to see you on your knees attempting to crawl.
That's why you play hide and seek.
For those who don't know, it's when you hide in the shadows,
put your goals in your pocket, but the ones that you are really trying to achieve.
No matter how hard it seems, never be afraid to chase your dreams!

Success
by Brieanna Dechesere

My eyelids are heavy, but my thoughts are heavier, I can't stop.
When you want success as much as you breathe, you might pop.
See I have goals in life, I can't be bought.
There's no price on this, what you thought?
When you get to the mountain don't you want to climb to the top?
My friends and family don't understand but it's not to be explained.
Everyone isn't always what they claim. But I know I didn't do it alone.
S is for the struggle, we all know it's real.
U is for the ultimate decision if you really want to go through with it.
C is for the compromise of social life.
C is for the commitment you have to stick with it and wait.
S is for the sanity you must keep.
S is for the Savior, without Him nothing is complete.
I work smart you can't compete.
But you can't get distracted by what's in these streets.

Ashleigh Baker

Alzheimer's
by Ashleigh Baker

Is my son here? No.
Is my son here? No.
Is my son here? No.
Where is he then? He is at work.
Every day, I take part in a cruel joke
Deceivingly telling my resident that her son is at work
When her son is actually deceased.
She is my honey, frail, always shaking, with snow white hair
I often find myself wondering what she was like before
Before she was diagnosed with Alzheimer's
She used to be a caregiver, a hard-working woman trying to support
her family
Her mind no longer processes
In a journal, she attempts to write - to remember,
but only "and, I, and, then, I wonder" are listed.
She always asks for her son until the sundowning takes place
By this witching hour, she is begging for forgiveness
Her son died in a car wreck - she was driving the car.
Is my son here? No.
He was my baby. I know ... he loves you.
Please bring him back ...
Honey, he will be back when you are

Emily Kombe

Freedom In a Box
by Emily Kombe

Filling out the form,
my hand, the color of "cafe con leche" as my mom says,
hovers indecisively over the African-American box.
"I am Zambian," I whisper to myself
Where the quickest up the curved mango tree gets to suck on its pit,
squatting above the warm compacted earth.
"I am Zambian," I say again, louder this time
My chest swells with pride, like a lion presenting a kill to its mate
I am powerful and strong like an elephant with full tusks
From the goatskin djembe and vibrantly colored chitenges.
But, I am also German, New English, and Danish.
These and many more simplified down to American.
I am first generation Zambian-American,
the first to check 2 boxes on the form.
I am mixed with more than just these two cultures.
I know there isn't a box that captures all of me
But I wish the box didn't confine me,
Didn't decide if I got in or not,
Didn't decide my race or background,
Didn't decide me.
You look at me, and guess I am African-American,
the correct box is clear to you.
"Yes," I say, but I am so much more than just the color of my skin,
so much more than just one box.

1st Place

Wilson Haims

Wilson is currently a sophomore in high school
and has spent her entire life on the coast of Maine.
She enjoys writing poetry and prose
inspired by her natural surroundings
and has an affinity for stories of all kinds.
Her submission, "A Season For Blueberries"
impressed even our toughest critics.
We consider it to be a wonderful piece of simplistic brilliance,
and are pleased to present it as our
2016 Winter Edition Editor's Choice Award Winner.
Congratulations, Wilson!

Editor's Choice Award

A Season For Blueberries
by Wilson Haims

We chewed gum the color of sunsets, wooden stairs rotting beneath us,
The trees seemed a black cityscape across the water.
It was a season for blueberries
A time when things of the same color cluster closely together
A time for a kitchen thick with the aroma of sweet, sticky pies
A time for us not only to be children,
but cowboys with brooms to call horses
and our fathers' broad leather hats
placed hastily atop our small heads.
We were kids–
minds swollen with the prospect of ourselves
as we romped wildly,
barefooted along the rocky shore,
toes sprawling in the late August water.
In the evenings my feet dangled
from our rust-studded dock
like over-ripened blackberries,
bursting with the juice that the sun left behind.
My eyes would always see the warm blush of the sunset as I dreamed,
my feet would feel the gentle clutch of the water,
and my mouth would taste
the final fresh winds of the season for blueberries.

Index
of
Authors

Index of Authors

Index of Authors

Index of Authors

Index of Authors

Imagine
Price List

Initial Copy 32.95

Additional Copies 25.00

Please Enclose $7 Shipping/Handling Each Order

Must specify book title and name of student author

Check or Money Order Payable to:

The America Library of Poetry
P.O. Box 978
Houlton, Maine 04730

Please Allow 4-8 Weeks For Delivery

THE AMERICA
LIBRARY OF POETRY

www.libraryofpoetry.com

Email: generalinquiries@libraryofpoetry.com